Macroeconomic Models

in a Causal Framework

Geoffrey J. Wyatt

Published by   *En Exempla Books*
                Harmony House
                Edinburgh EH10 4SD
                U.K.

The moral rights of the author have been asserted.

ISBN: 0-9546202-1-6

http://geoffwyatt.com

Macroeconomic Models
in a Causal Framework

CONTENTS

Preface

The purpose of this book is pedagogical, in the widest sense. It will have achieved its aim if it persuades readers of the usefulness of a causal, graphical representation of economic models, and encourages them to formulate and write down economic models in flowgraph representations. The graphical techniques presented here complement the traditional representations of economics by adding an explicitly causal perspective. I believe a causal perspective deepens our appreciation and understanding of the models we use in economics.

Macroeconomics is a natural application area for this approach because it is a system science: it comprises linked components, *i.e.* interacting markets, institutions and government policies. Models which represent all these elements are necessarily complex and open to various interpretations depending on what is considered to be exogenous or endogenous. In fact those very words already contain the notion of causality, so an explicitly causal approach is quite appropriate.

Who should read this book? Well, I would say anyone who wants to learn more about macroeconomic models. It can accompany and complement most textbooks in macroeconomics,[†] though it is not itself a macroeconomics textbook. It does not try to cover the gamut of macro economics, and in particular does not examine modern optimising representative agent models. Nor does it examine factor markets, though a causal approach is quite applicable there too; nor economic growth. But, used as an accessory or supplement to an intermediate macroeconomics textbook, students will find a new perspective on many of the models presented there, and perhaps discover some unexpected implications. The book should also be useful to those engaged in the formulation or analysis of fiscal and monetary policies, by providing new ways to understand and explain their effects.

[†] Such as, among the many excellent texts now available, those by: Mankiw; Dornbusch, Fischer and Startz; Hall and Taylor; Blanchard; Burda and Wyplotz; and De Long.

The material in this book has been used as the core of a class in macroeconomic modelling for some ten years now, and I am grateful to the many students and class tutors who have enabled me to refine my ideas, and occasionally brought me down to earth, over that period of time. That class follows a standard intermediate level macroeconomics class, but it does not build on it in the sense of starting where the earlier material left off. Rather it goes back over the now familiar ground again *ab initio*, but using the flowgraph representation. That may be why it has also been a successful vehicle for teaching macroeconomics to MBA students, especially those with a background in engineering.

The level of mathematics needed to master the material presented here is no more than is usually assumed for a class in intermediate macroeconomics; in other words, the basic algebra of linear equations together with some understanding of the basic concepts of differential calculus. In fact only basic algebraic manipulations are needed to solve flowgraphs in this book. But certain presentational decisions were made to keep things simple. In particular it was decided to employ a discrete time formulation for dynamic models, using the lag operator, and then only to consider two aspects of model solutions, namely immediate effects and long-run effects, ignoring the transition path between these states. This meant that the whole apparatus of Laplace- or z-transforms could be avoided. Although transitional dynamics arises naturally in engineering, it is of much less relevance in economics which has rather little to say about disequilibrium.

Long before I had the opportunity to teach this material I doodled with flowgraphs, learned from colleagues in control engineering, simply as a means of explaining macro models to myself. It was only when I came to use them in seminar settings that I appreciated that other people, students and colleagues, could also use them to advantage. That is why I began to teach macroeconomics in this way, and why I have written this book: behold the models!

Geoffrey Wyatt
Edinburgh
2004

1

Introduction:
Causal Representation

1.1 The causal framework

The notion of cause and effect is deeply engrained in our understanding of the world. It also has profound and sometimes controversial resonances in philosophy, which will be side-stepped in this book. From a philosophical standpoint the attitude here is that causal reasoning and causal representation help us to understand and analyse many topics in macroeconomics. In other words, causality is conceived here as a pedagogical tool for explication of the matter in hand, both to ourselves and to others.

Economists are generally ambivalent about causal arguments. On the one hand such arguments are used extensively in the classroom where we quite often find a form of homespun causal representation produced on the blackboard. But on the other hand causal arguments are often eschewed in the more formal writings of economists. The reluctance to use explicitly causative arguments is probably based on two different reasons, one stemming from the analytical side and the other from the empirical side of the subject.

On the analytical side, economists are most confident about statements to do with equilibrium configurations of the economy but are generally less confident about transitions between equilibria, or the mechanisms by which the equilibria are established. On the empirical side, analysis often falls into the realm of econometrics, which has historically been heir to the skepticism about causality to be found in its other parent discipline, statistics.

The standard methodology of comparative statics in economic analysis illustrates the power of reasoning based on notions of equilibrium. The archetypal example is of supply and demand in some market, in which equilibrium is synonymous with equality between supply and demand. Allow some external condition to change and we get a new equilibrium which can be compared with the original one. For example "bad weather spoiled the harvest and reduced supply so that there is a higher price and lower quantity transacted in the new equilibrium". This is fine, but wouldn't a causal explanation require us to know exactly how the new equilibrium was established? On this topic economists often appear ill at ease, perhaps justifiably.

The mechanism by which the price was driven up may be obscure without knowledge of the institutional and other conditions governing behaviour in this market. The precise details of disequilibrium behaviour depend on circumstances, and as they are often unknown it may be thought better to reason without recourse to such arguments: whatever the circumstances, the equilibrium can be described, so it is safer to keep to that. Nevertheless, it is clear where the causal chain began—with the bad weather—and where it ended, with the rise in price. So although we might not be able to fill in the details, at least the status of these two variables, as cause and effect, is not in doubt despite the many conceivable routes between them. To arrive at this overarching causality, it is sufficient to assert that price rises when demand exceeds supply.

The empirical source of the unease with causal reasoning stems from statistics and is crudely summarised by the true statement that correlation does not imply causation. This, combined with the fact that economists are seldom in a position to conduct controlled experiments, inclines them to follow the statisticians in the tradition begun by Karl Pearson and assume a skeptical stance with regard to causation[†]. The correlation/causation point is often sharpened for economists by the "identification problem" which heavily qualifies the conditions under

---

[†] see J. Pearl, *Causality* (Cambridge University Press, 2000) and K. D. Hoover, *Causality in Macroeconomics* (Cambridge University Press, 2001) for extensive discussions.

which an empirical association between jointly determined endogenous variables can be ascribed to one mechanism of that joint determination or another. Nevertheless, econometricians as much as anybody are keen to explore causal relationships, and have developed sophisticated methods, both for testing the direction of causality in time series data and for coherently estimating components of simultaneous structural models.

In the classroom, where the need for causal argumentation is irresistible, we often find an appealing but incomplete causal representation in a kind of visual shorthand. To illustrate, consider what might be seen on the blackboard after a class on monetary policy:

$$Ms\uparrow \rightarrow i\downarrow \rightarrow r\downarrow \rightarrow I\uparrow \rightarrow Y\uparrow \rightarrow Md\uparrow \rightarrow i\uparrow$$

This is a wonderfully compact summary of the argument that an increase in the money supply induces a fall in the rate of interest which induces a rise in investment which raises total expenditure and income, which in turn raises the demand for money which pushes the interest rate up. A horizontal arrow could stand for "implies", but more naturally means "causes", while the vertical arrows show the direction of change of the associated variable. But the point here is that the (horizontal) arrow schema is a primitive representation of "causality". Primitive, both in the sense of being crude and unrefined, and also in the sense of being a foundation building block. It does the job of identifying cause and effect, and indeed of displaying a causal chain. However, its shortcomings in this regard are also easily apparent: the illustrated causal chain reveals a contradiction—or at least an incompleteness—in that it shows the rate of interest initially falling but then rising. Then what is the eventual effect of increased money supply on the rate of interest? And furthermore, since the chain could obviously be extended by repeating its last four links, *ad infinitum*, how can any conclusion be reached?

Now we come to the point of this book. Its aim is to present some models in macroeconomics, making use of the vivid "homespun" causal representation of the classroom blackboard, but doing so in a systematic and coherent manner. The vehicle we use to achieve this aim is known in some branches of engineering as a "signal-flow graph", but here it is simply referred to as a "flowgraph".

1.2   Flowgraphs

The representation of an engineering system, with its various transforming devices and mechanisms, as a graph is quite normal. The graph
abstracts and displays the essential structure of the system being modelled. Such a graph may often appear similar to an electric circuit diagram, with its representation of the sundry connected physical elements.
When the graph represents a more general system it is known as a
"block diagram", in which each block represents some mechanism
which transforms input variables into output variables. Textbooks on
control engineering and systems engineering are replete with such block
diagrams. Variables are conceived as flowing along the connecting lines
between the transforming blocks just as electric current might be
thought to flow along the wires of an electric circuit, transformed *en
route* by resistors, inductors and so on. The block diagram representation also appears in economics textbooks, showing the circular flow of
income. But there is another graphical representation in which the
blocks, or "nodes" now, are the variables and the connecting lines between them represent the transformations. This "signal-flow graph", or
more simply "flowgraph", easily and naturally represents linear equations, in which case the transformations on the connecting lines are
coefficients or simple multipliers.

Flowgraphs and block diagrams are alternative, dual, representations
of the same real system. A visual advantage of the block diagram is its
physical resemblance to the system being modelled, whereas a visual
advantage of the flowgraph is its transparent causal interpretation. In
what follows there will be many applications of flowgraphs to macroeconomic models, but first we must find out how they are constructed,
manipulated and analysed.

1.3   Building flowgraphs: basic operations

Suppose that variable X causes variable Y, and that we write down the
relationship thus:

$$Y = f(X) \tag{1}$$

This representation reads "Y is a function of X", seeming to imply that Y is determined by X, or caused by X. But of course the algebraic representation does not itself imply a direction of causation. The relationship could just as easily be written

$$X = f^{-1}(Y) \tag{2}$$

where the function $f^{-1}(\ )$ is the inverse of $f(\ )$. The mathematical representation is agnostic about the direction of causality. But if we know that X causes Y, then equation (1) seems more meaningful than equation (2).

Let us be more specific and suppose that Y is proportional to X, so that:

$$Y = aX \tag{1a}$$

where a is a constant. Of course, this is algebraically equivalent to:

$$X = Y/a \tag{2a}$$

and the equation representation remains agnostic as to causal direction. But consider now writing the linear proportional relationship (1a) in manner which does show the direction of causality.

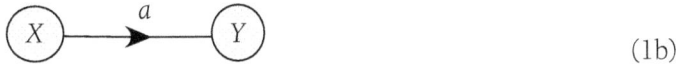

$$\tag{1b}$$

This reads "X causes Y with transmittance a". Instead of an equation, (1b) depicts the relationship between Y and X as an "elementary graph". The arrowed line is a "directed edge", and a directed graph is made up of a set of such directed edges connecting various nodes. Note that we also represent the transmittance—or "gain" in engineering parlance—between X and Y as a. This type of graph is known to systems engineers as a "signal flow graph", or simply a "flowgraph".

Observe that the graph incorporates more information than an equation because it displays the direction of causation, which is crucial for a cognitive interpretation. But, it might be thought, equations have the advantage that they can be manipulated and solved. In fact, graphs too can be manipulated and solved. Moreover, graphical manipulations themselves convey more insight into the system they represent than do the corresponding algebraic manipulations, and solving for the effect of one variable on another is much simpler for a flowgraph than for the corresponding equations. This is particularly true for qualitative solutions.

Because graphs contain more information than equations, the relationship between them is not one-to-one. Many graphs may be implied by one equation, but there will only be one graph that is consistent with a particular causal interpretation of that equation. We now examine graphs involving more than one directed edge or arc, and how they can be simplified. The five parts of Figure 1.1 illustrate different features of graph construction and simplification, and the corresponding equations.

In part (i) we see the basic property of path transmittances: that the overall transmittance is the product of the individual arcs comprising the path. Part (ii) shows that the total effect on a node is the sum of the effects from all its inflowing arcs. These two properties are combined in part (iii) to show that the overall transmittance from X to Y is the sum of the two distinct paths between these nodes. It is evident from this flowgraph representation of "arcs in parallel" that there is just one exogenous variable in this system, namely X, whereas that fact is somewhat opaque in the equations even if the left hand side variable of each equation is designated the "dependent variable".

When a system includes a feedback process of some description, its flowgraph will contain a loop, as shown in part (iv) of Figure 1.1. Here Y depends on X and Z, but Z in turn depends on Y. Algebraically this is treated as a system of "simultaneous equations", without further ado, though the very notion of simultaneity begs questions about causality and dynamics in the system it represents. A loop occurs when some path emanating from a node (*i.e.* a variable) eventually returns to that same node. Here there is a "loop transmittance" of bc. It is quite possible for a node to be on several distinct loops, which may or may not have an arc or arcs in common. Distinct loops which include the same nodes are said to be "touching", as in part (v). As will be seen, it is important to know whether loops are touching or non-touching when it comes to solving for some overall transmittance between two nodes. Here there are two loops which have nodes Y and Z in common, and are therefore touching. It can be seen that if the lower loop were simplified by absorbing the W node there would then be two simple feedback paths in parallel from Z to Y which could be consolidated to produce a flowgraph with just one feedback loop having a loop transmittance equal to $b(c+ed)$.

i. Arcs in cascade $Z = aX$ $Y = bZ$ $\Rightarrow \quad Y = abX$	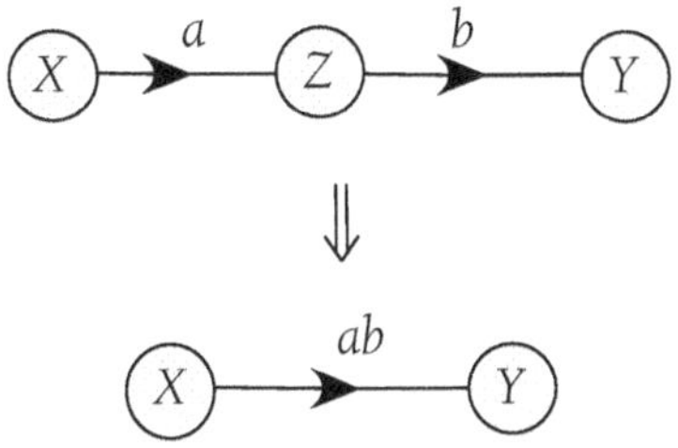
ii. Summation $Y = aX + bZ$	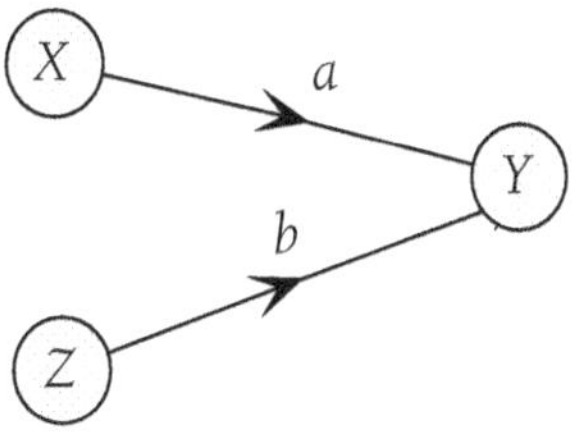
iii. Arcs in parallel $W = aX$ $Z = cX$ $Y = bW + dZ$ $\Rightarrow Y = (ab + cd)X$	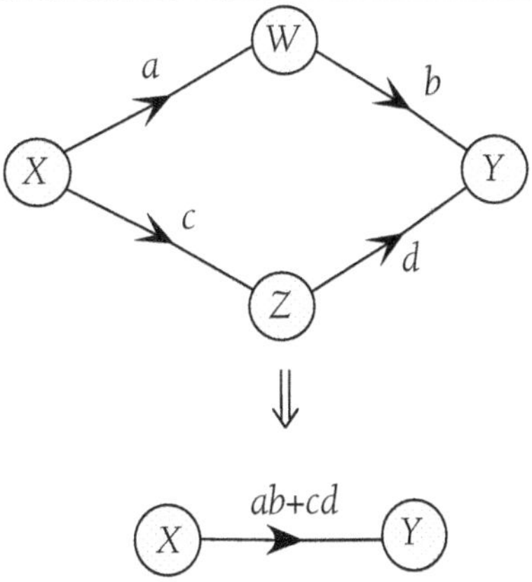
iv. Loop $Y = aX + cZ$ $Z = bY$	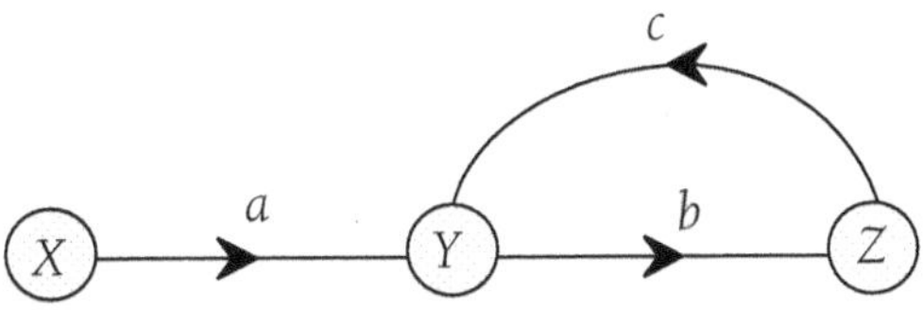
v. Touching loops $Y = aX + cZ + dW$ $Z = bY$ $W = eZ$	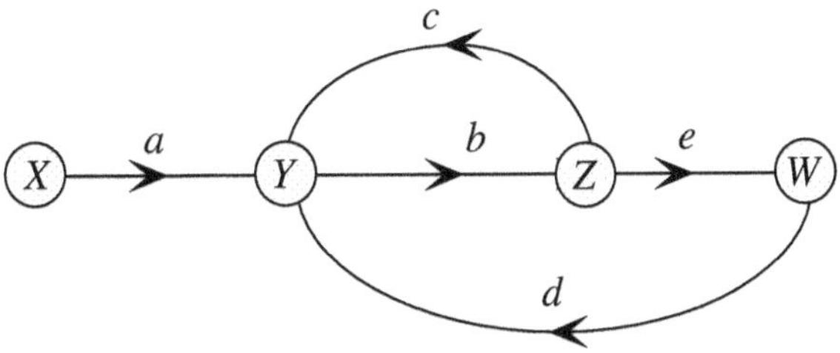

Figure 1.1 Equations and graphs

1.4   Condensing a graph

The process of condensing a graph is equivalent to the algebraic process
of substituting from one equation into other equations. The basic operations involve the combination of arcs in parallel (see above), the
elimination of intermediate nodes with arcs in cascade, the reduction of
loops involving several nodes to "self loops" on one of those nodes, and
the absorption of self loops.

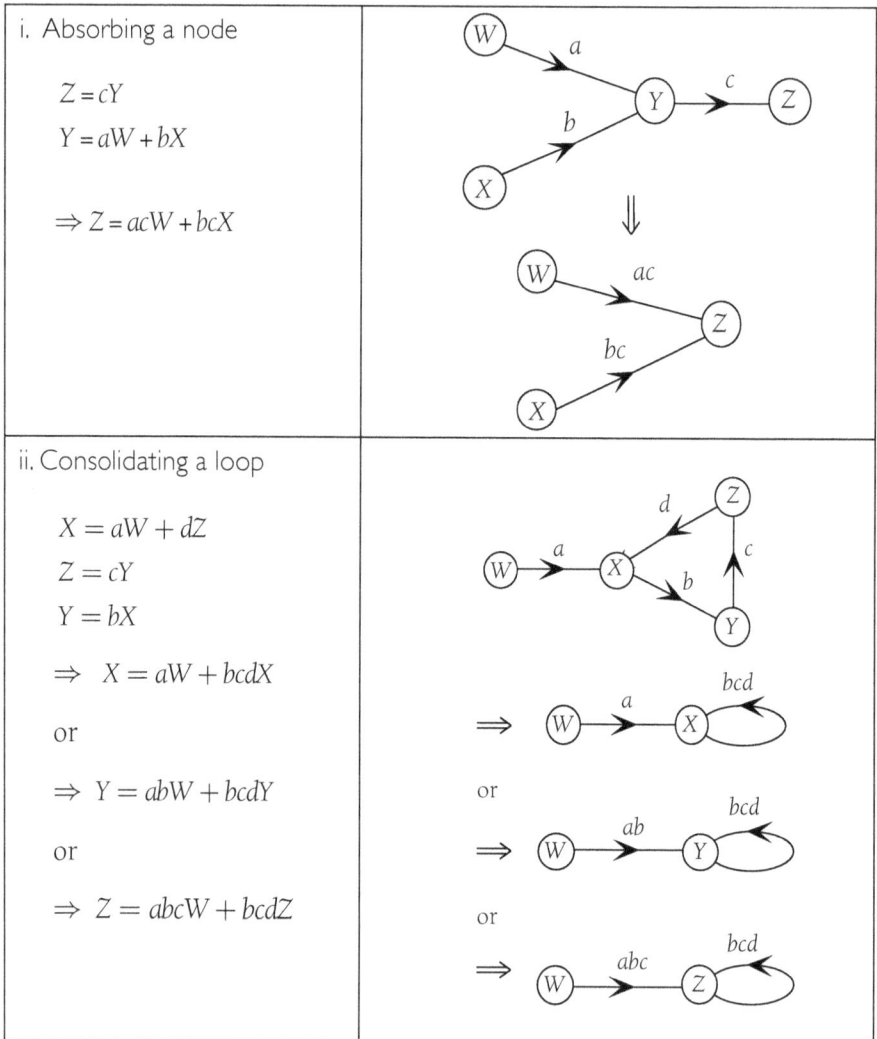

i. Absorbing a node $Z = cY$ $Y = aW + bX$ $\Rightarrow Z = acW + bcX$	
ii. Consolidating a loop $X = aW + dZ$ $Z = cY$ $Y = bX$ $\Rightarrow\ X = aW + bcdX$ or $\Rightarrow Y = abW + bcdY$ or $\Rightarrow Z = abcW + bcdZ$	

Figure 1.2 Effects of node absorptions

Figure 1.2(i) illustrates the effect of node absorptions. The procedure is simply to remove the node from the flowgraph, but in doing so to retain all the path connections between the remaining variables along with their path transmittances.

All loops can be reduced to self-loops on one of the variables within the loop by a sequence of node eliminations, as illustrated in Figure 1.2(ii). Any variable within the loop can act as the self-loop node. Note that the loop transmittance is not affected by the choice of node variable upon which to focus the loop. Thus in the example shown, the three-node loop can be reduced by three different sequences of node absorptions. The loop transmittance is always the same, and the path transmittances between the remaining variables are unaltered.

By these means, all loops can be reduced to self loops. Moreover, all self loops can be absorbed into the direct paths that lead into a node, as shown in Figure 1.3.

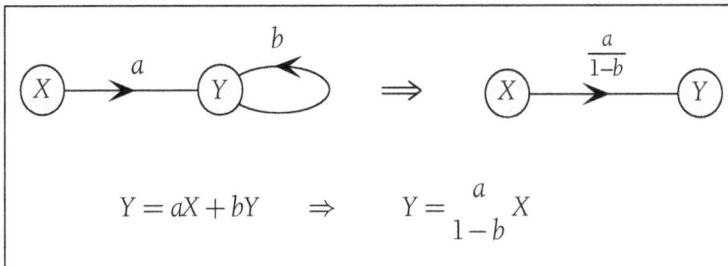

$$Y = aX + bY \quad \Rightarrow \quad Y = \frac{a}{1-b}X$$

Figure 1.3 Absorption of self loop into inflowing arc

The limiting reduction of a graph produces the *reduced form* of the model, in which all the paths are direct connections from source nodes (exogenous variables) to sink nodes (endogenous variables). The reduced form has an important role in econometrics, where it contrasts with the structural form of a model which expresses our understanding about how the model works in its detailed components. The reduced form hides those details but reveals the overall cause and effect roles of the variables—the magnitudes of those effects are the transmittances associated with the arcs.

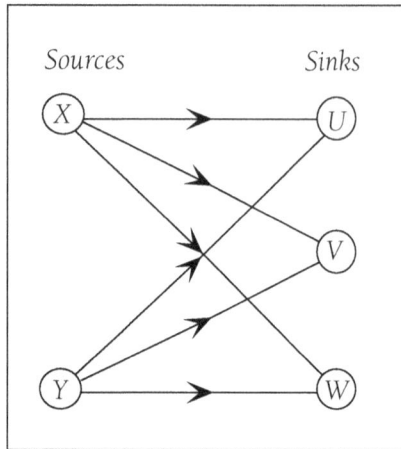

Figure 1.4   Reduced form

1.5   Evaluation of transmittances

i.   Direct paths

We often wish to calculate the effect of a change in an exogenous variable on one or several endogenous variables. In a flowgraph, an exogenous variable is recognised by the fact that it only has outflow arcs emanating from it. Any variable with an inflow arc is endogenous, even if it also has outflows. Where there are no loops in the flowgraph it is straightforward to calculate the overall transmittance from an exogenous to an endogenous variable. All that needs to be done is to identify all the paths connecting the two nodes, calculate the transmittance along each of them and add them up. Consider the flowgraph in Figure 1.5.

There are two exogenous variables, U and V, and all the other variables are endogenous. Note that there is no path connecting V to X, so V cannot affect X and thus the transmittance between them is zero. Consider the transmittance between V and Z. It is simply egd, since only arcs in cascade are involved. Now consider the transmittance between U and Z. There are three direct paths, and the overall transmittance is, accordingly, $a + bcd + bfgd$.

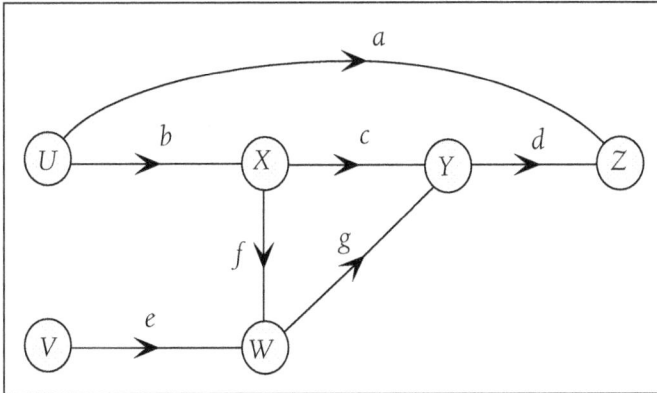

Figure 1.5   Direct paths

It is perhaps instructive to consider the same model written out as equations:

$$X = bU$$
$$W = eV + fX$$
$$Y = cX + gW$$
$$Z = aU + dY$$

These equations have been written down in a particular order to show the structure of the model. It is evident that if we are given the values of the exogenous variables, U and V, the system can be solved from top to bottom by substitution, i.e. the system is "recursive" in the sense given to that term by the Swedish economist Herman Wold. The same point can also be made by expressing the model in matrix form, with the endogenous variables on the left hand side and the exogenous variables on the right hand side:

$$\begin{pmatrix} 1 & 0 & 0 & 0 \\ -f & 1 & 0 & 0 \\ -c & -g & 1 & 0 \\ 0 & 0 & -d & 1 \end{pmatrix} \begin{pmatrix} X \\ W \\ Y \\ Z \end{pmatrix} = \begin{pmatrix} b & 0 \\ 0 & e \\ 0 & 0 \\ a & 0 \end{pmatrix} \begin{pmatrix} U \\ V \end{pmatrix}$$

where the thing to note is the lower triangular structure of the matrix of coefficients of the endogenous variables. When a flowgraph has no loops, the matrix of coefficients on the endogenous variables can always be written in lower triangular form.

ii.   Paths with loops

The advantages of flowgraphs are also evident in models that contain feed-back mechanisms—*i.e.* flowgraph models with loops. If we wish to evaluate the transmittance between an exogenous and an endogenous variable in such a flowgraph, there are two ways to go about it. Firstly we could use the methods of graph reduction outlined above, until the graph shows a single arc connecting the variables we are interested in. Alternatively we can use a formula known as Mason's rule.

To use Mason's rule we need to extract the following information from the flowgraph: (i) all the direct transmittances from the exogenous variable to the endogenous variable, *i.e.* all the T_i, where i indexes the set of paths connecting the variables, and (ii) all the loop transmittances in the system, L_j, indexed by j. Let the overall transmittance we seek be labelled T, then Mason's rule is:

$$T = \frac{1}{\Delta}\sum_i T_i \Delta_i$$

where Δ, which is the "system determinant", and the "cofactor" terms Δ_i are evaluated in terms of the various loop transmittances. They are given by:

$$\Delta = 1 - \sum_j L_j + \left[\sum_{k,l} L_k L_l - \sum_{k,l,m} L_k L_l L_m + ...\right]_{nontouching\ loops}$$

and Δ_i is the value of Δ excluding all terms which involve loops which touch the ith forward path (*i.e.* set the value of such touching loop transmittances to zero).

The term $\sum_k L_k L_l$ is the sum of the products of all pairs of non-touching loop transmittances, and similarly the term $\sum L_k L_l L_m$ is the sum of the products of all loop transmittances for all possible combinations of three non-touching loops. The term in square brackets goes on to include similar terms for combinations of four, five *etc.* non-touching loops until the possible combinations are exhausted. This usually occurs well before we reach combinations of four non-touching loops, thankfully! Consider the example shown in Figure 1.6.

In this flowgraph there are two forward paths from U to Z, with transmittances $T_1=abcde$ and $T_2=afe$ respectively. There are three loops, with transmittances $L_1=cg$, $L_2=feh$, and $L_3=bcdeh$, and the loops L_1 and L_2 are non-touching, so the system determinant is:

$$\Delta = 1-(L_1+L_2+L_3)+L_1L_2$$
$$= 1-cg-feh-bcdeh+cgfeh$$

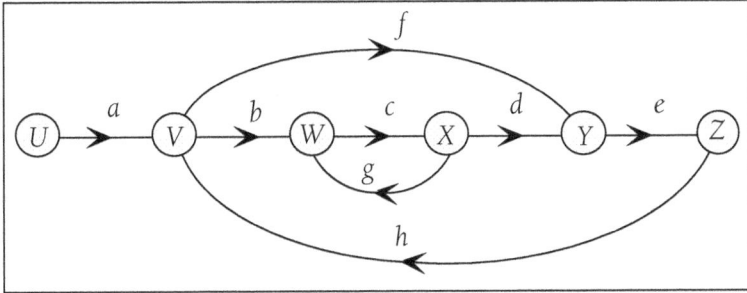

Figure 1.6 Flowgraph with loops

Because all three loops touch path T_1, setting $L_1=L_2=L_3=0$ in the expression for Δ gives $\Delta_1=1$. Because loops L_2 and L_3 touch path T_2, setting $L_2=L_3=0$ in the expression for Δ gives $\Delta_2=1-L_1=1-cg$. These results can now be substituted into Mason's formula to get the overall transmittance from U to Z as:

$$\left\langle \frac{Z}{U} \right\rangle = \frac{T_1\Delta_1 + T_2\Delta_2}{\Delta} = \frac{abcde + afe(1-cg)}{1-cg-feh-bcdeh+cgfeh}$$

where the left hand side has been expressed as a ratio in angle brackets to signify "transmittance". The context determines how to interpret transmittance.

If the model is static and linear then the transmittance represents the ratio of the change in Z to the change in U, *ceteris paribus*—i.e. holding the other exogenous variables constant. If the model is static and non-linear, so that the arc transmittances $a,b,c,...etc.$ represent partial derivatives, the flowgraph represents a local linear approximation and the overall transmittance can be interpreted as the total derivative dZ/dU, which is strictly only valid for small changes. Finally, if the model is linear and dynamic, so that the system contains dynamic operators, such as lags or time derivatives (represented by the Laplace transform operator), the overall transmittance represents the "transfer function" from U to Z.

Now let us see how our model can be solved by expressing it in matrix notation and using the usual Cramer's rule. From the flowgraph we can write down the following equations:

$$V = aU + hZ$$
$$W = bV + gX$$
$$X = cW$$
$$Y = dX + fV$$
$$Z = eY$$

which can be expressed in matrix terms, with endogenous variables on the left as:

$$\begin{pmatrix} 1 & 0 & 0 & 0 & -h \\ -b & 1 & -g & 0 & 0 \\ 0 & -c & 1 & 0 & 0 \\ -f & 0 & -d & 1 & 0 \\ 0 & 0 & 0 & -e & 1 \end{pmatrix} \begin{pmatrix} V \\ W \\ X \\ Y \\ Z \end{pmatrix} = \begin{pmatrix} a \\ 0 \\ 0 \\ 0 \\ 0 \end{pmatrix}(U)$$

so Cramer's rule gives the solution for Z as:

$$Z = \frac{\begin{vmatrix} 1 & 0 & 0 & 0 & aU \\ -b & 1 & -g & 0 & 0 \\ 0 & -c & 1 & 0 & 0 \\ -f & 0 & -d & 1 & 0 \\ 0 & 0 & 0 & -e & 0 \end{vmatrix}}{\begin{vmatrix} 1 & 0 & 0 & 0 & -h \\ -b & 1 & -g & 0 & 0 \\ 0 & -c & 1 & 0 & 0 \\ -f & 0 & -d & 1 & 0 \\ 0 & 0 & 0 & -e & 1 \end{vmatrix}} = \frac{abcde + afe(1 - cg)}{1 - cg - feh - bcdeh + cgfeh}U$$

which is the same result as before, but derived by way of tedious and error-prone algebra.

1.6   Modelling with flowgraphs: further topics

Here we discuss certain topics which arise in the context of modelling with flowgraphs, namely (i) qualitative flowgraphs, (ii) dynamics, (iii) parameter variation and (iv) reversal of causality.

i   Qualitative flowgraphs

The "qualitative calculus" is a characteristic of comparative static analysis. It is easily and naturally accommodated within a causal flowgraph representation. Although the flowgraphs set out above represent linear systems with algebraic parameters, those parameters could be taken to be the partial derivatives of non-linear functions for which the linear formulation serves as a local approximation. It is usually the case in economics that our theoretical understanding of the components within the system is "non-parametric", often comprising monotonicity assumptions rather than more precise assumptions about functional form. Then the true information in the flowgraph is of the *signs* of the parameters. For this reason it is useful to maintain a convention that all the algebraic parameters shown on a flowgraph are positive, so that a negative effect is signified by a minus sign in an arc transmittance. This convention enables an immediate inference about the direction of change in an endogenous variable induced by a change in an exogenous variable: the task is merely to identify the signs of all the paths connecting the two variables. This can be seen on inspection in graphs that are not too complicated. Of course in a situation in which two such paths have path transmittances with different signs, the overall impact on the endogenous variable is ambiguous.

Systems which contain loops may appear to pose a problem for this simple procedure for the sign calculus. That could indeed be so in some unusual cases, but usually the loops can be ignored for the purpose of signing effects. An important constraint on the ability of loops to upset the simple calculation is that the systems we consider are assumed to be stable. This implies that the system determinant is positive, so the denominator in Mason's rule formula cannot change the sign given in the

numerator. By itself this is not sufficient to justify the simple sign calculus based on the path transmittances because a negative path cofactor
could reverse the sign of the term in the numerator of Mason's rule. So
as a precaution we should identify any loops that do not touch the path
concerned (and any such non-touching pairs etc), and mentally check
whether the cofactor could conceivably be negative—a warning sign
would be non-touching loops with loop transmittances exceeding one in
value. If this seems possible, then it would be wise to do the algebra on
the numerator in Mason's rule. But in the relatively simple models we
shall encounter that is seldom necessary.

ii.   Dynamics

There is a close connection between a causal understanding of a system
and its dynamic behaviour. Whenever we consider a static model there
are dynamics lurking not far below the surface. But they are often un-
charted territory for economics and as such best avoided. However from
a causal perspective it is often useful to recognise them. For example,
the simple market supply and demand model only concerns equilibrium
states, but an explanation about how the system gets from one such
state to another can hardly avoid bringing in dynamics (*e.g.* "excess
demand stimulates a rise in the price"). A causal understanding of the
system hinges crucially on implicit or explicit dynamics. Static models
usually represent an equilibrium state of an underlying dynamic system,
and the implicit dynamics can come in various guises. Perhaps the most
common is the assignment of exogeneity to particular variables. This
tells us what changes first, even though algebraically we consider the
system to be simultaneous.

    The very notion of "simultaneity" means that the time-scale at which
our flow variables are represented is much larger than that at which the
dynamic process of influence from one variable to another operates. If
we could write down the model with sufficiently fine granularity in
time, we would find that all the arcs in the model embody lags or accumulations. For most models such detail would be an inessential distrac-
tion at best, but at worst would result in complete obfuscation. We

would not be able to see the wood for the trees. Sometimes, however, the essence of a model's behaviour is in its dynamics, which therefore must be represented explicitly. This actually helps in the construction of the flowgraph because it is natural to assume that the past causes the future rather than the reverse.

The analytical tools needed for a dynamic model depend on the characterisation of time: as continuous or discrete. This determines whether the equations of the model are represented as differential or difference equations. Either form of dynamic equation can be presented and analysed within a flowgraph representation, but since the stronger tradition in economics is that of discrete time, the dynamic models here are formulated in discrete time as difference equations. In practice this means that the models may contain the lag operator L. Where it is encountered, L should be treated as an algebraic parameter. This means that in the flowgraph representation of dynamic models certain arcs will have an arc transmittance involving L, or quite often $(1-L)^{-1}$ which implies accumulation or time-integration.

For example, consider a model in which the rate of change of p (the logarithm of the price level) is inversely proportional to u (the rate of unemployment): $\Delta p = p_t - p_{t-1} = -au$. With the use of the lag operator, this translates into $p(1-L) = -au$, or

$$p = \frac{-au}{1-L},$$

allowing the elementary graph representation depicted in Figure 1.7.

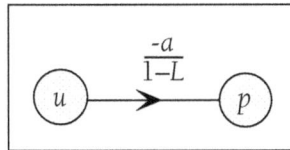

Figure 1.7 Dynamic arc

iii.   Parameter variation

It is often of interest to consider the implications of some parameter within an overall transmittance taking a particular value. This is espe-cially so for the lag operator L, because L =0 corresponds to the "short-run" outcome while $L = 1$ corresponds to the "long-run" or "equilibrium" outcome. Consider the latter case. Often the overall transmittance will be a ratio in which both the numerator and the denominator may contain terms involving $(1–L)^{-1}$. Then it is usually helpful to re-express the transmittance by multiplying both the numerator and the denominator by $(1–L)$ before setting $L=0$ or $L=1$. This avoids "infinities".

Zeros and infinities in individual arc transmittances alter the topography of the flowgraph. When an arc transmittance goes to zero the flowgraph is simply modified by removing that arc. But the more interesting and more difficult case is when an arc transmittance goes to infinity. Then the only paths that matter are the loops and transmittances which include that arc because its effect dominates all others. It is often the case that an arc transmittance which goes to infinity is part of a loop. Then we restrict attention to those paths whose transmittances T_i or cofactors Δ_i include that arc, because otherwise the path transmittance would effectively go to zero. Similarly we consider only those loops or non-touching loop pairs that contain the arc. In the example of Figure 1.6 above, let $b \to \infty$, then the direct path from U to Z that bypasses node W can be ignored and similarly the two loops, between W and X and between V, Y and Z, can be ignored. Thus Mason's gain formula for the transmittance from U to Z becomes $abcde/(1–bcdeh)$ which simplifies to $–a/h$ on dividing both numerator and denominator by the infinitely large b.

iv.   Reversal of causality

This means that at least one variable which was previously considered to be endogenous is now made exogenous. That is to say, its value is fixed outside the model. For each such variable whose role has changed another, previously exogenous variable, must now be considered endogenous, with its value determined by the system under study. Of course we could just go back to the equations, and manipulate them so that the new set of endogenous variables appears on the left-hand side, and construct a revised graph from the equations. But it is also possible to manipulate the existing graph directly.

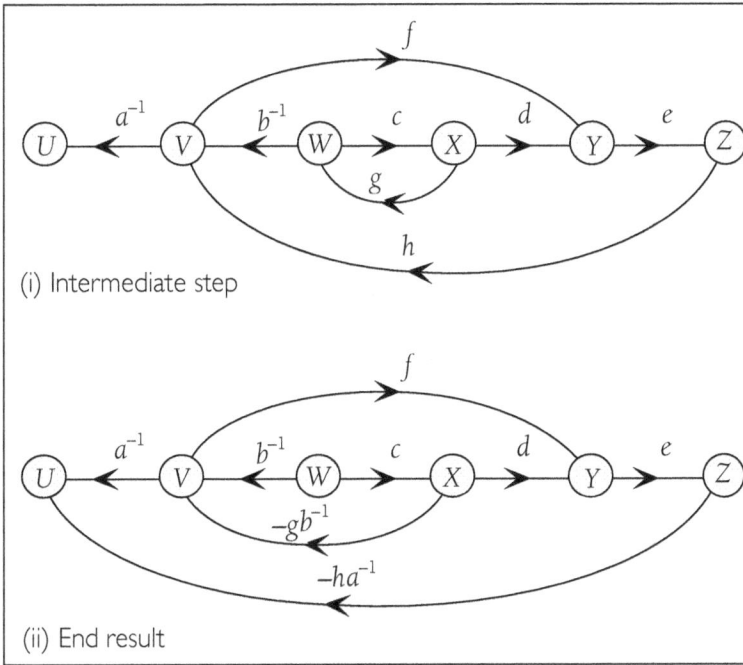

(i) Intermediate step

(ii) End result

Figure 1.8 Reversal of causality

This is illustrated in Figure 1.8 which reverses the causality between the W and U nodes of the flowgraph of Figure 1.6. The procedure is as follows: first select the two variables whose roles are to be reversed and find a path connecting the two nodes (if there is more than one such path, then a choice must be made and the eventual outcome graph will not be unique); next reverse all the arrows of the arcs along that path and invert all the associated arc transmittances; next change the sign of the transmittance of any arc that converges onto any node in the new path; finally shift the end points of all these converging arcs to the next node in the new direction, preserving the new transmittances to those nodes.

1.7 Brief bibliography

The representation of linear models as flowgraphs was introduced into the world of systems engineering by Samuel Mason in the following papers.

S. J. Mason, "Feedback theory: Some properties of signal flow graphs," *Proc. IRE*, vol. 41, pp. 1144-1156, Sept. 1953.

S. J. Mason, "Feedback theory: Further properties of signal flow graphs," *Proc. IRE*, vol. 44, pp. 920-926, July 1956.

The techniques of flowgraph manipulation and solution are discussed in many textbooks of control systems analysis, including the following as representative examples.

B. C. Kuo, *Automatic Control Systems*, 7th ed., 1995, New York: Prentice Hall.

R. C. Dorf, *Modern Control Systems*, 8th ed., 1998, New York: Addison Wesley.

F. H. Raven, *Automatic Control Engineering*, 5th ed., 1995, New York: McGraw Hill International.

J. J. D'Azzo and C. H. Houpis, *Linear Control Systems Analysis and Design*, 4th ed., 1995, New York: McGraw-Hill

R. T. Stefani, C. J. Savant Jr., B. Shahian and G. H. Hostetter, *Design of Feedback Control Systems*, 3rd ed., 1994, Boston: Saunders College Publishing.

C. S. Lorens, *Flowgraphs for the Modeling and Analysis of Linear Systems*, 1964, New York: McGraw-Hill.

Of these, Kuo's is the most extensive presentation, and in it he emphasises the fact that Mason introduced the signal-flow graph as a cause-and-effect representation. But the connection to a causal interpretation appears to be of minor importance to most modern control systems engineering textbooks, which see the advantages of the flowgraph representation firstly as a more elegant and simpler picture than the block diagram, secondly as a means of solution via Mason's rule as an alternative to step-by-step reduction of block diagrams, and thirdly as a vehicle for the representation of state space methods in systems of differential equations. The short monograph by Lorens is the source of the causality reversal technique outlined in this chapter.

2

Output and Expenditure

We begin with static models of the real economy at the aggregate level, abstracting from money, prices, international linkages and economic growth. Our causal perspective depends on what we consider to be held fixed, or exogenous. In the *short-run* the output of the economy is determined by the level of expenditure, which is made up of three components: private consumption, investment and government spending. These components of expenditure are in turn determined by variables like taxes and the real interest rate, which are considered to be exogenous. This is the "Keynesian" perspective. But in the *long-run* output is exogenous, being determined by the level of employment of the factors of production: capital and labour. This is the "classical" perspective, in which the real interest rate adjusts to bring expenditure into line with the given level of output.

An issue that arises under both the long- and the short-run is how to treat the public sector balance, or the government financing constraint. Without a financial sector in the model there is no mechanism to accumulate debt, so strictly speaking the government budget must be balanced. From a long-run perspective this is as it should be, but should a balanced budget be imposed in the short-run too? It could be argued that if the financial consequences of a government surplus or deficit have little impact on the real economy in the short-run, they can be ignored. Below we present the simple short-run model in both versions, with an unbalanced budget and with a balanced budget. The different consequences show how important the assumption is.

2.1   IS model with taxes in the short-run

A linear version of a simple standard textbook model of the real macro economy comprises the following equations:

$$E = C + I + \bar{G} \tag{1}$$

$$Y = E \tag{2}$$

$$C = C_0 + cY^d \tag{3}$$

$$Y^d = Y - T \tag{4}$$

$$T = T_0 + tY \tag{5}$$

$$I = I_0 - a\bar{R} \tag{6}$$

where E is expenditure, Y is total output or GDP, C is consumers' expenditure, I is investment, G is current spending by the Government, Y^d is disposable income, T is taxes and R is the real interest rate. A bar over a variable indicates that the variable is exogenous, and variables labelled with zero subscripts—intercepts—are "shift parameters" or "exogenous shocks" to the equations in which they appear.

A flowgraph of the IS system is displayed in Figure 2.1. It is constructed by assuming that the left-hand side variable in each equation is determined by that equation. Our causal understanding is only ambiguous about the income-expenditure "identity" (1), but since each component of expenditure is determined by the other equations in the system, it is only the total that can be determined by that equation. Thus the topography of the flowgraph is uniquely determined by our causal understanding of the model. How the graph is actually laid out is a matter of choice: the principal criterion should be its intelligibility. In the case of Figure 2.1(b), the layout was selected bearing in mind the intention to add on a graph of the LM system later.

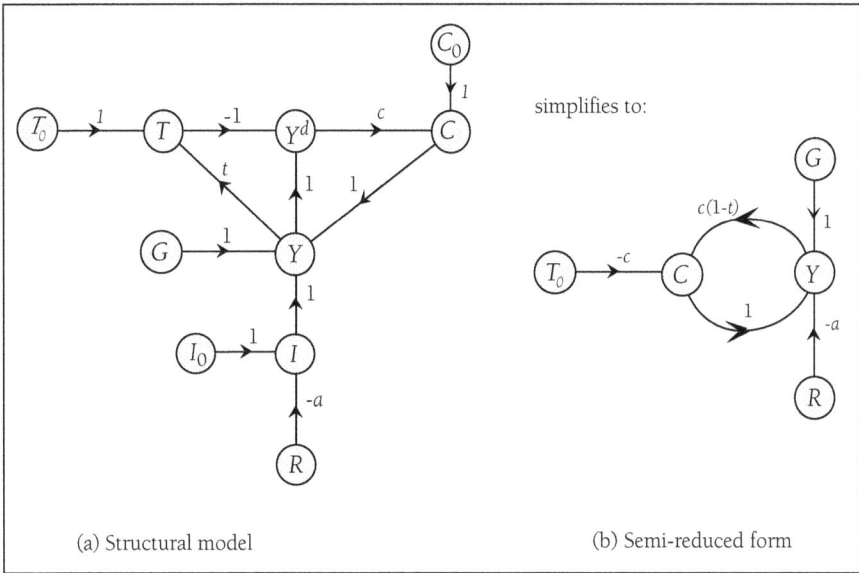

(a) Structural model   (b) Semi-reduced form

Figure 2.1 The IS subsystem

The flowgraph in Figure 2.1(a) displays the full detail of the model from the causal transcription of the equations. However, in practical work it is desirable to keep only the essential detail needed for the purpose in hand, and by absorbing the intermediate variables T, Y^d and I according to the rules set out in Chapter 1, and ignoring the shift parameters I_0 and C_0, the flowgraph simplifies to that shown in Figure 2.1(b), where the one loop $L=c(1-t)$ implies the system determinant $\Delta=1-c(1-t)$, and Mason's rule immediately gives the familiar Keynesian multiplier formulae:

$$\frac{dY}{dT_0} = \frac{-c}{1-c(1-t)}, \quad \frac{dY}{dG} = \frac{1}{1-c(1-t)}, \quad \frac{dY}{dR} = \frac{-a}{1-c(1-t)}$$

$$\frac{dC}{dT_0} = \frac{-c}{1-c(1-t)}, \quad \frac{dC}{dG} = \frac{c(1-t)}{1-c(1-t)}, \quad \frac{dC}{dR} = \frac{-ac(1-t)}{1-c(1-t)}$$

The standard diagrammatic representation of the IS system as found in macroeconomics textbooks (the "Keynesian cross") is reproduced as Figure 2.2.

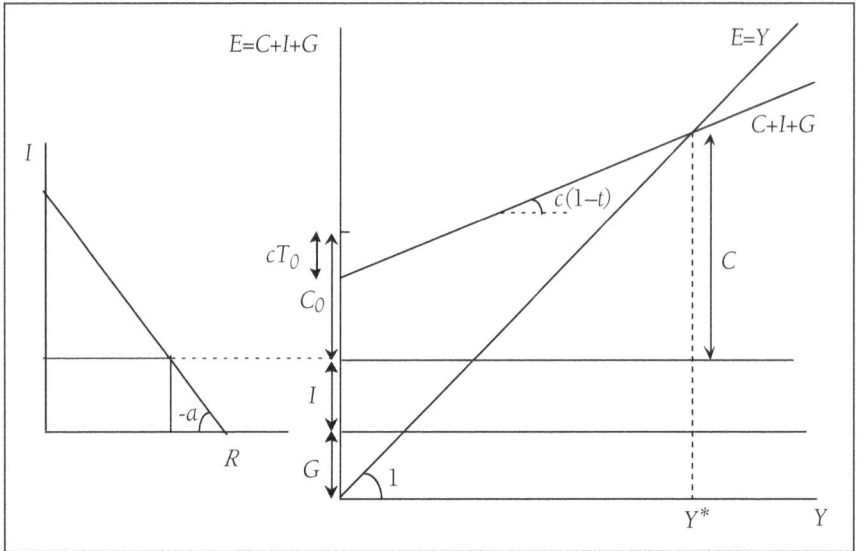

Figure 2.2 The "Keynesian cross" diagram

Note that the axes of the diagram on the right represent the two endogenous variables, C and Y of the flowgraph of Figure 2.1(b), and that the slopes of the two lines in the Keynesian cross diagram are given by the arc transmittances $C{\rightarrow}Y$ and $Y{\rightarrow}C$ of that flowgraph.

Now conduct the following thought experiment. Suppose that the real interest rate R is reduced by one unit (one percentage point, say), and examine the consequences for the equilibrium level of output Y^*. The $C+I+G$ line shifts upward by the induced change in investment, a. It now crosses the $E=Y$ line further to the right. But how much further? It is not easy to see from the diagram, which only gives us a qualitative answer (Y^* increases). But the transmittance calculation from the flowgraph does give the result, as $a/(1-c(1-t))$, which could also be obtained from the equations by algebra. It turns out that this is a key transmittance in the larger IS-LM system to be derived below: it is the absolute value of the slope of the IS curve in R-Y space. To emphasize this, Figure 2.3 shows the reduced form of the IS flowgraph with only Y and exogenous variables as nodes, juxtaposed with the IS curve.

The reduced form flowgraph of Figure 2.3 shows how GDP is determined by the exogenous variables in the IS system. In particular we see that changes in R induce changes in Y with transmittance $-a/(1-c(1-t))$. Y varies inversely with R, and the covariation of Y and R traces out the IS curve on the right in Figure 2.3. Changes in government spending and taxes produce horizontal shifts in the IS curve.

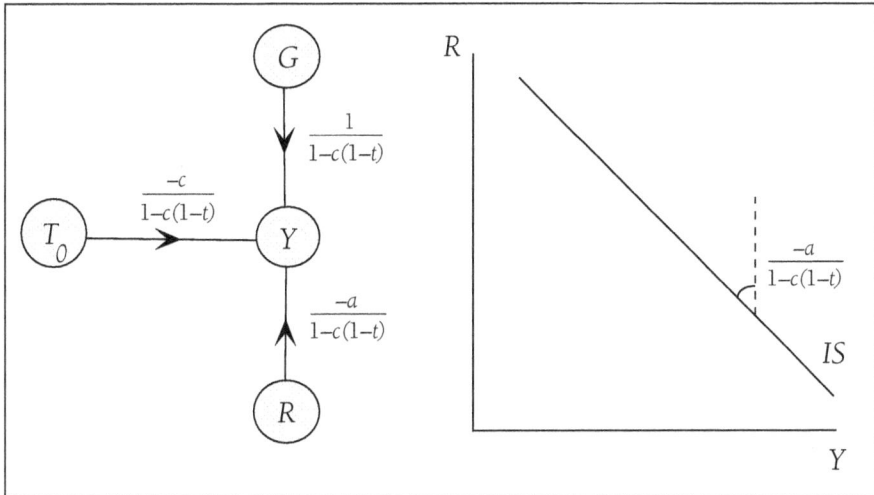

Figure 2.3 The IS curve

Exercise 1

In the IS model of section 2.1, replace the linear tax function with a simple lump-sum tax: $T = \bar{T}$. Redraw the flowgraph and evaluate the transmittances from exogenous variables to the endogenous variables. Condense the flowgraph to display just C, G, R, T and Y.

2.2   Dynamics in the IS model

The model of Section 2.1 is of an equilibrium system. However any explanation of what happens when an exogenous variable changes is bound to involve dynamics. For example, an unplanned change in stocks (inventories), persuades producers to reduce output if stocks increase or to increase output if stocks fall. It is not difficult to bring stocks or inventories explicitly into the model, but for simplicity we merely replace the equilibrium condition, equation (2), with the following simple dynamic adjustment equation:

$$Y = LE \ ,$$

which says that output is equal to expenditure in the previous period.

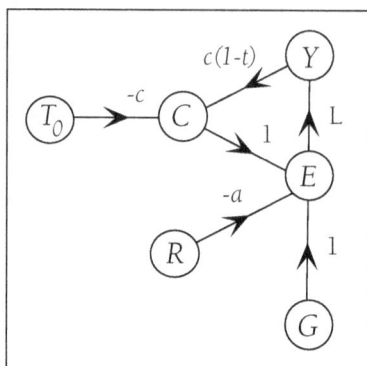

Figure 2.4 IS model with simple dynamics

The system determinant is $\Delta = 1 - Lc(1-t)$. Using Mason's rule we derive the transmittances implied by the model, for example the transmittance from autonomous taxes to GDP:

$$\left\langle \frac{Y}{T_0} \right\rangle = \frac{-cL}{1 - Lc(1-t)} \quad \xrightarrow{L=0} \quad 0 \quad \text{in the short-run, and}$$

$$\xrightarrow{L=1} \quad \frac{-c}{1 - c(1-t)} \quad \text{in the long-run.}$$

The long-run corresponds to "equilibrium", and we see that this agrees with the result of Section 2.1.

Exercise 2

Find all the long- and short-run transmittances from T_0, G and R to C, E and Y.

2.3   Short-run IS model with a balanced budget

In the absence of a monetary or financial sector the government is unable to escape from the need to balance its budget. The obligation to match public spending with tax receipts is known as the government's budget constraint. It has the effect of changing the topography of the flowgraph of the model by introducing a connection between taxes and government spending. But how they are connected depends on the *manner* in which the budget is balanced. There are several ways in which a balanced budget can be achieved. The government could balance its budget by adjusting the fixed element of taxes, or by changing the marginal tax rate t, or by adjusting the level of government spending. The connections in the flowgraph and the behaviour of the model depend upon which of these means is used to achieve budgetary balance. Here we examine two scenarios: (a) the government treats T_0 as fixed and adjusts G to balance the budget, and (b) the government treats G as fixed and adjusts T_0 to balance the budget.

We keep the same equations as those of the model of section 2.1 except that the interest rate is omitted for simplicity and an equation for the balanced budget is introduced:

$$Y = C + I + G \qquad \text{income equals expenditure;}$$
$$C = C_0 + c(Y\text{-}T) \qquad \text{consumption function;}$$
$$T = T_0 + tY \qquad \text{tax function;}$$
$$G = T \qquad \text{balanced budget.}$$

These equations give rise to different flowgraphs depending on which variables are assumed to be exogenous.

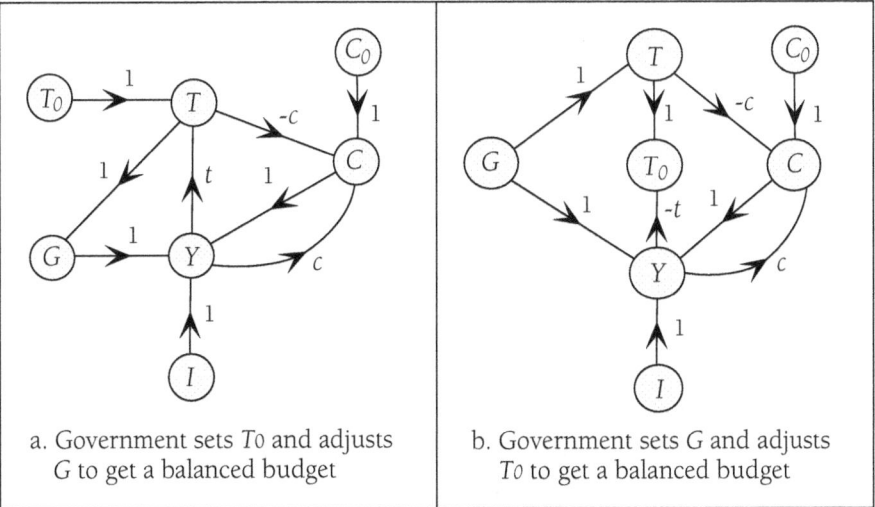

a. Government sets T_0 and adjusts   b. Government sets G and adjusts
  G to get a balanced budget T_0 to get a balanced budget

Figure 2.5 Balanced budget models

Note that the flowgraph on the left has three loops, while that on the right has just one. This affects the "system determinant"—*i.e.* the denominator in the formula of Mason's rule. Another important difference between these flowgraphs is the set of paths between variables. Note that on the left there is just one path from G to Y, whereas on the right there are two.

Exogenous variables.	Endogenous variables		
	dY	dT	dC
dI	$\dfrac{1}{(1-c)(1-t)}$	$\dfrac{t}{(1-c)(1-t)}$	$\dfrac{c}{(1-c)}$
dC_0	$\dfrac{1}{(1-c)(1-t)}$	$\dfrac{t}{(1-c)(1-t)}$	$\dfrac{1}{(1-c)}$
dT_0	$\dfrac{1}{(1-t)}$	$\dfrac{1}{(1-t)}$	0

Table 2.1 Multipliers (transmittances) in Model (a)

Exogenous variables.	Endogenous variables		
	dY	dT	dC
dI	$\dfrac{1}{(1-c)}$	0	$\dfrac{c}{(1-c)}$
dC_0	$\dfrac{1}{(1-c)}$	0	$\dfrac{1}{(1-c)}$
dG	1	1	0

Table 2.2 Multipliers (transmittances) in Model (b)

Several interesting comparisons can be made. Firstly, note that the transmittances ("multipliers") are quite different from those of the model of Section 2.1. Secondly, by comparing Tables 2.1 and 2.2, it can be seen that the "GDP multipliers" from shocks to investment and consumption are affected by the manner in which the government balances its budget. Model (a) generally has the larger multipliers, however the consumption multipliers are not affected by the budget balancing scheme. Thirdly, the tables confirm that Haavelmo's celebrated balanced budget result—that

GDP and government spending change by equal amounts—holds irrespective of how the budget balance is brought about (recall that $dT=dG$ in these models). To see this in model (a) where both T and G are endogenous, note that $dY=dT$ ($=dG$) when T_0 changes.

With the help of the flowgraph, let us consider why consumption is quite insensitive to changes in taxes and government spending in these balanced budget models. In Model (a) there are two paths from T_0 to C, with equal and offsetting transmittances. An increase in autonomous taxes raises total taxes, thereby depressing disposable income, but the increase in total taxes also raises government spending, and thereby GDP by an equal amount, so there is no net effect on disposable income. Hence consumption cannot change. A similar story can be told for Model (b), beginning with a change in government spending.

Exercise 3

i.   How does a balanced budget affect the slope of the IS curve?

ii. Add an equation for government spending, $G = G_0 + gY$ to the model of this section and modify Figure 2.5b to create a flow-graph in which I, C_0 and G_0 are exogenous. Construct a table of multipliers for this model and compare them with those of the model of Fig. 2.5b.

2.4 Long-run IS model

What should be understood by the terms "long-run" and "short-run" depends upon the context. Often the term "long-run" refers to the steady-state equilibrium of a dynamic system, while in a different context, usually microeconomic, the term could refer to a state in which all factors of production are variable. In the present context the long-run is a state in which output is at full capacity, constrained by the given factor inputs, so it applies to the trend state of the classical macroeconomy, abstracting from the business cycle. Thus output and expenditure are pinned down, exogenous. But equilibrium in the IS model still implies that output equals intended expenditure (or intended savings equals intended investment), though this cannot now be brought about by variations in aggregate demand; instead it is brought about by adjustment of the real interest rate.

Figure 2.6(a) is essentially the same as Figure 2.5(b), but with a couple of extra nodes to give a bit more detail. It represents the Keynesian "short-run" in which total expenditure adjusts to bring about equilibrium in the system. By contrast, although Figure 2.6(b) represents the same equations, it displays a flowgraph with causality reversed between GDP and the real interest rate.

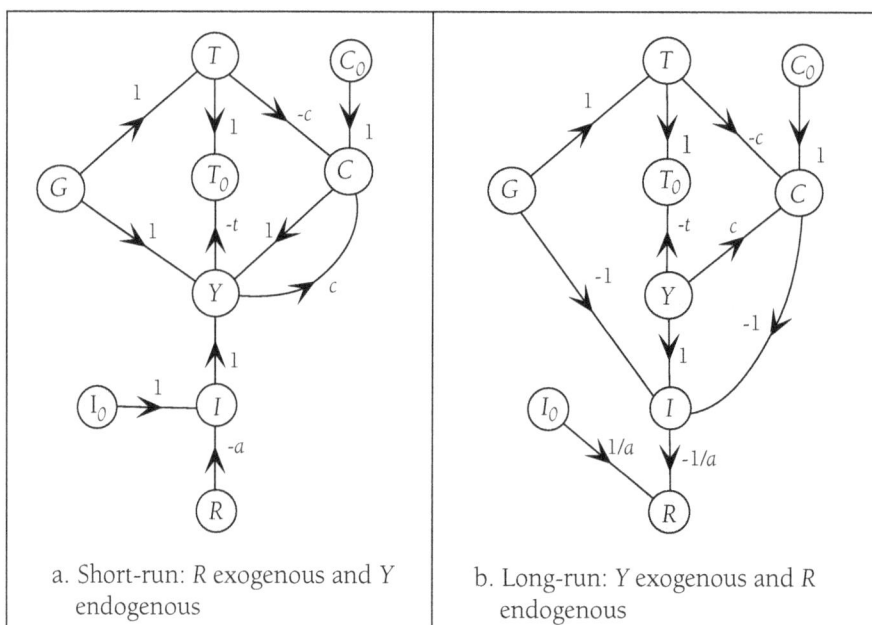

a. Short-run: R exogenous and Y endogenous

b. Long-run: Y exogenous and R endogenous

Figure 2.6 Causality reversal in the IS model

The long-run interpretation of the IS model is in effect a version of the classical loanable funds theory. With total output (and expenditure) given, an increase in government consumption G or in private consumption C_0 must reduce savings, and also investment. The interest rate has to rise in order to bring investment down to this lower level of savings. Also, with a given level of savings, a rise in autonomous investment I_0 pushes up the real interest rate. Thus, with total output exogenous, a rise in any of the components of aggregate demand in-creases the interest rate. But an increase in output, although it must raise private consumption and investment, will push the real interest rate down.

Exercise 4

i.   Ascertain for yourself that the two flowgraphs of Figure 2.6 imply the same equations. Also, check that the flowgraph procedure for causality reversal enables 2.6(b) to be derived from 2.6(a).

ii. Give an explanation of the long-run IS model in terms of a tradi-tional "supply and demand" type of diagram, with the interest rate on the vertical axis and savings and investment on the hori-zontal axis.

iii. Suppose that the consumption function depends on the rate of interest, $C = c(Y–T) – bR$. How does this affect the short-run sen-sitivity of Y to changes in G in the model of Figure 2.6(a)? How does it affect the long-run sensitivity of R to changes in G in the model of Figure 2.6(b)?

3

The Money Market

3.1   Private sector liquid assets

Private sector wealth is the value of all assets owned by citizens of the country as individuals. It excludes those assets which they own collectively, i.e. public sector assets such as public roads and parks, military hardware and so on. People decide on the proportions of their assets to hold in different forms. We distinguish financial assets from non-financial assets. A financial asset held by one citizen is a claim for future payment(s) to be made by other citizens, for whom the claim is a liability. As such they net out for society as a whole, and it is only real assets that contribute to real wealth. But financial assets are important for the functioning of the economy. Among the many different kinds of financial assets, there are two categories that are particularly important because of their influence on the economy. These are assets which are created by the government, namely money itself and government securities. Government securities—bonds and bills—represent claims on future tax income. When they were issued they enabled the government to meet a shortfall in taxation to finance its activities of the day. At any moment the private sector holds a stock of such bonds and bills which the government has issued in the past. The private sector also holds a stock of money in the form of notes and coins issued by the central bank, by which the government has also acquired resources from the private sector in the past, but this time without a promise to repay anything in the future.

Although the causes and consequences of government financing is an interesting topic of itself, our present focus is on the way in which the central bank as the government's agent can manipulate the proportions of these two forms of government-created paper assets. It does this through "open market operations". If the central bank wishes to decrease the stock of money held by the private sector it simply issues new government securities which individuals purchase by paying cash or writing cheques against their private bank accounts. The money used to buy the securities is thus transferred to the central bank and is removed from circulation. In this way open market sales of government securities reduce the stock of money. The new securities issued by the central bank for this purpose are usually short-dated "treasury bills". Similarly, if the central bank wishes to increase the stock of money held by the private sector it would simply buy government securities on the open market, writing cheques against itself as payment. Such cheques are equivalent to the issue of new notes and coin, and can be exchanged for such by the commercial banks which receive them as deposits. Of course the terms on which the public are persuaded to buy or sell government securities have to be acceptable. This may mean that the government's broker has to offer treasury bills at a lower price, or bid for them at a higher price than the prices at which they currently trade in the market.

Money is held either as cash—notes and coins—or as bank deposits. Let us suppose that the public wishes to hold cash and deposits in the proportions c and $1-c$ respectively. Now, bank deposits may be held either as demand deposits in checking accounts or as time deposits in deposit accounts. Let us suppose that the public wishes to hold demand deposits and time deposits in the proportions d and $1-d$ respectively. We can envisage the immediate consequences of a government sale of treasury bills, i.e. a withdrawal of money from the economy, as shown in Figure 3.1.

The sale of treasury bills has reduced private sector liquid assets by an equal amount, of which proportion c is a reduction in cash and proportion $1-c$ is a reduction in bank deposits. Within the reduction in bank deposits a proportion d comes from demand deposits and proportion $1-d$ comes from time deposits. Note that while the total of private sector liquid assets has declined, there has been no change in the pro portional composition of that total.

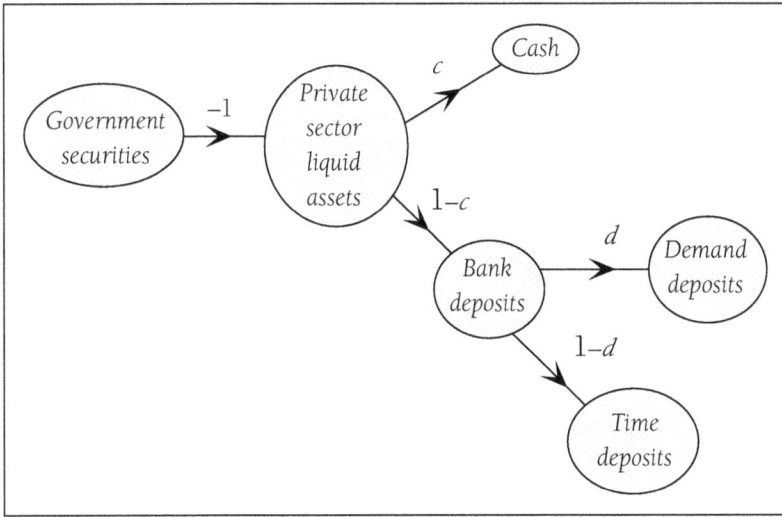

Figure 3.1 Private sector liquid assets

3.2   Banks, the money multiplier and the money supply

Thus far we have treated the banks simply as passive recipients of deposits. This is obviously incomplete. Banks not only hold private sector deposits, which are their liabilities, but they also have assets in the form of loans to the private sector as well as reserves comprising deposits with the central bank and vault and till cash with which to meet withdrawals. The important point is that on the asset side of their business it is the loans which provide income to the commercial banks. However not all deposits can be loaned out to borrowers. A fraction, r, must be retained in the bank as reserves to meet withdrawals by depositors. In some countries there is a legal minimum for r, but in others it is at the discretion of the banks which are expected to act prudently. However, the main function of modern banks is one of financial intermediation, being a channel between lenders and borrowers. When they use their deposits as the basis for prudent lending, the private sector recipients of these bank loans are provided with an immediate increase in their liquid assets in exchange for an obligation to repay over some future period. Thus a bank loan increases the total stock of private sector liquid assets. The process continues when the recipient of the loan—the borrower—

uses it to pay suppliers, who in turn deposit these payments into their own bank accounts, enabling the banks to make more loans, which further increases the stock of private sector liquid assets. Thus the banking system creates both credit and deposits, *i.e.* money. This is shown in Figure 3.2 as a flowgraph by incorporating the banks' division of their deposits between loans and reserves into the earlier picture of Figure 3.1.

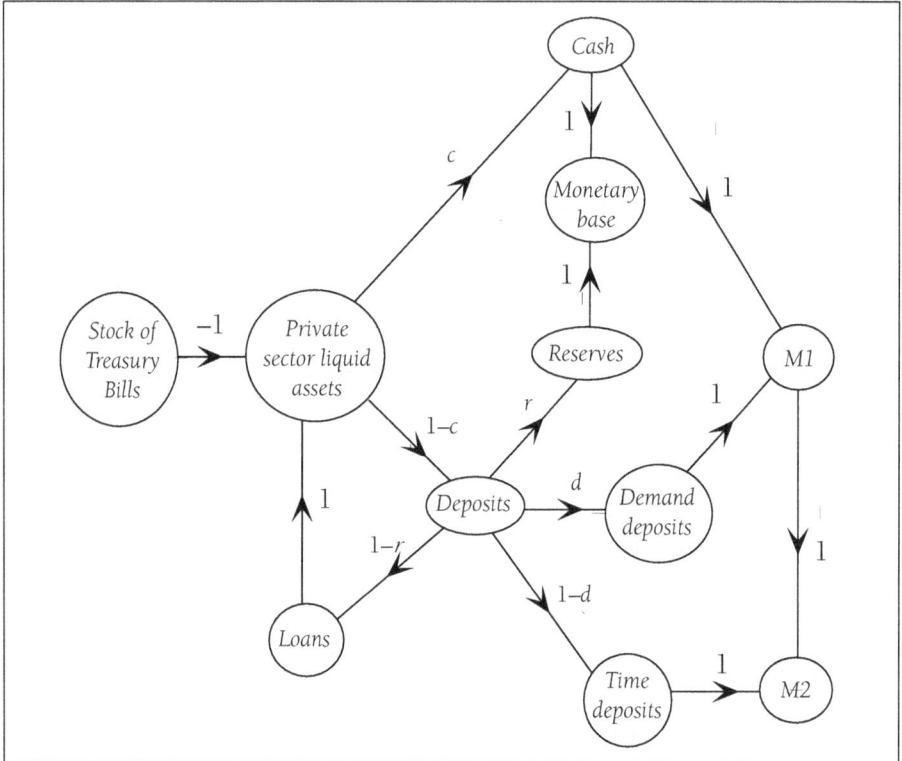

Figure 3.2 Money supply and the banking system

What is called the "monetary base" also goes under the name "high powered money". It is the sum of cash and bank reserves. The narrow money supply M1 is the sum of cash and demand deposits, and the wider money supply M2 is obtained by adding time deposits to this. The new parameter introduced in this flowgraph is r, the "reserve ratio", *i.e.* the proportion of deposits that are kept as bank reserves. Note that c

here is the proportion of private sector liquid assets held as cash, and not the ratio of cash to deposits, which is often used instead. The flow-graph shows that if there is a change in private sector liquid assets, the ratio of cash to deposits is maintained at $c' = c/(1-c)$. For the time being we consider c, r and d as fixed parameters, but in fact they may all vary with interest rates. The implications of this are considered below.

The flowgraph allows us to write down various money multipliers on inspection. There is one loop, with loop transmittance $L = (1-c)(1-r) = 1-c-r+r.c$, and all paths stemming from the treasury bill purchase touch that loop. Thus, applying Mason's rule, we find:

$$\Delta H = \frac{-c-(1-c)r}{c+r-r.c} \Delta TBills = -\Delta TBills$$

which tells us that the monetary base, or "high powered money", H, decreases one for one when open market operations increase the stock of treasury bills held by the public, i.e. with sales of treasury bills by the government broker. We can also derive the effects on the money supplies M1 and M2:

$$\Delta M1 = -\frac{c+d(1-c)}{c+r-r.c} \Delta TBills$$

$$\Delta M2 = \frac{-1}{c+r-r.c} \Delta TBills$$

This final expression gives the famous "money multiplier" which is the ratio of $\Delta M2$ to ΔH. (Note that the usual textbook expression of the money multiplier is often expressed in terms of c', the ratio of cash to deposits, instead of c, the proportion of cash in private sector liquid assets. However, we can see the equivalence:

$$money\ multiplier = \frac{1}{c+r-r.c} = \frac{1+c'}{c'+r} \quad since \quad c = \frac{c'}{1+c'})$$

The flowgraph illustrates a narrative account of the consequences of an open market operation. Consider how the money supply increases. The government purchases treasury bills or bonds from the public by issuing cheques drawn on its account at the central bank. This increases the stock of liquid assets held by the public, of which a proportion c is kept in the form of cash and the remainder is held in bank deposits, divided between demand deposits and time deposits. The bank matches its increased deposit liabilities with assets, split between loans and reserves at the central bank, in the ratio $(1-r):r$, where r, the reserve ratio is determined by banking prudence, possibly constrained by government regulation. The loans made to the public add to the private sector's stock of liquid assets, which is identical to the broad money stock, M2. Thus the flowgraph can be collapsed to the reduced form:

$$-\Delta TBills \xrightarrow{m} \Delta M2$$

where m is the money multiplier, $m = (c+r-r.c)^{-1}$.

Now the "parameters" r and c in the money multiplier actually depend on the level of interest rates, and so therefore does m. The more interest people can earn on their bank deposits the less cash they wish to hold as part of their liquid assets, so c is negatively related to interest rates. Moreover, the higher are interest rates, the more costly are banks' holdings of reserves which do nor bear interest, so r also falls as interest rates rise. Although, it is often the case that government stipulates a minimum below which r cannot fall, even then the negative relation with interest rates will still hold for the "excess reserves" above that minimum. This is the case in the United States for example, where excess reserves are a key feature in the analysis of the money supply process. These considerations lead to the implication that the higher are interest rates the greater is the money multiplier.

Although the government can determine the monetary base H by open market operations, if it wishes to steer the economy by controlling a stock of money it needs to determine a wider measure of money than H: one that is used for transactions purposes, like M2. This means that it must know the behaviour of the money multiplier m, which is determined by the preferences of the public for cash, represented by c, and the preferences of the commercial banks for reserves represented by r. In order to do this it must know how c and r depend on interest rates and how interest rates, which depend on the state of the whole economy, are going to behave. This may be a tall order, as the experience of governments in setting, and often failing to achieve, monetary targets bears out.

The foregoing implies a money supply function of the following kind:

$$M^s = m(i)H$$

in which the money multiplier m is an increasing function of the nominal interest rate i. Although we cannot be more precise than this about $m(i)$ it is convenient to represent it as:

$$m(i) = e^{m_0 + m_1 i} \quad \text{or} \quad \ln m(i) = m_0 + m_1 i$$

where m_0 and m_1 are positive parameters. We may consider this to be a tractable approximation which allows us to write the money supply function in terms of the logarithms of the money stock variables:

$$m^s = m_0^s + m_1 i + h \tag{1}$$

where m^s is the logarithm of the money supply, $\ln M^s$, and h is the logarithm of high powered money, $\ln H$. Shocks and trends in the money supply such as those due to financial innovations which make access to money more convenient can be captured by allowing the "constant" m_0^s to change over time. The parameter m_1 is the "interest semi-elasticity" of money.

3.3   Demand for money

The demand for money stems primarily from its use as a medium of exchange. Thus we expect it to be held in proportion to the value of transactions per unit of time. Hence the price level and a measure of the volume of transactions are important determinants of the amount of money people wish to hold. On the other hand money yields no intrinsic utility—or so it is often thought—but it has a cost in the foregone yield of alternative assets, so people will economise on their money holdings. The demand for money is therefore assumed to be determined by three factors: it should be proportional to the price level; it should vary inversely with the opportunity cost of holding money; and it should vary directly and roughly proportionally with a scale variable standing for the volume of transactions. One way to model the effect of the price level on the demand for money is to formulate the demand for money in terms of real money balances. But in this chapter we assume that the price level is constant, so this factor can be ignored. The opportunity cost of holding money is well approximated by the yield on alternative riskless assets, *i.e.* the interest rate on bonds. Although we are considering a fixed price level, so that real and nominal interest rates are identical, in the more general setting in which they differ the appropriate measure of the opportunity cost of holding money is the nominal interest rate. The appropriate scale variable is often assumed to be the level of output or total income in the economy, but a reasonable alternative that has some empirical support is consumer expenditure. For the moment we assume that GDP is the appropriate scale variable. Thus we may express the demand for real money balances as:

$$\frac{M^d}{P} = L(\underset{+\ -}{Y,i}) \quad \text{or} \quad M^d = P.L(\underset{+\ -}{Y,i})$$

where Y is real GDP, i is the nominal interest rate and P the general price level, which for now is assumed to be constant. The label for the money demand function, L, stands for "liquidity", which is the key attribute of money, and indeed the demand for money is also called "liquidity preference".

To be more specific we could assume a linear money demand function, which would have the virtue of simplicity, though a preferable formulation which conforms with many empirical studies of the demand for money, would have a constant scale elasticity and a constant interest semi-elasticity:

$$m^d - p = m_0^d + \beta_1 y - \beta_2 i \tag{2}$$

in which m^d is log(M^d), the scale variable y is log(GDP), p is log(P) and m_0^d is a shift parameter or shock to the money demand function. Note that i, the nominal interest rate on government bonds, is not log-transformed.

3.4 Equilibrium in the money market

Let us first of all assume that the supply of money does not depend on the interest rate. This assumption is quite common. Then, stipulating that the money market is in equilibrium, we have the following system:

$$M^s = mH$$
$$M^d = P.L(Y,i)$$
$$M^s = M^d$$

in which H and Y are exogenous and P is constant. This has a unique causal structure since H causes M^s, and the equilibrium requires M^d to be equal to M^s, so i is determined by the money demand equation. This is shown in the qualitative flowgraph of Figure 3.3.

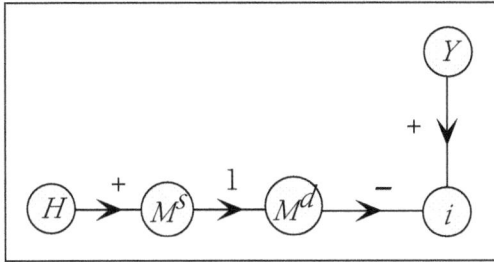

Figure 3.3 The LM subsystem

Since this flowgraph only represents a state of equilibrium in the money market, it does not strictly have an interpretation as a sequence of causes and effects. It states, for example, that if the stock of high powered money H is increased, that increases the supply of wider money, and to maintain equilibrium this implies that the demand for money has to increase. For this to be achieved, given that income is exogenous, the interest rate must fall. Similarly, if income Y rises the interest rate must also rise in order to keep the demand for money equal to the unchanged supply of money.

Let us now incorporate the positive dependence of the supply of money on the interest rate into this structure. Thus we replace the money supply equation with:

$$M^s = m(i).H$$

Starting with Figure 3.3, we need to add an arc with positive transmittance going from i to M^s. This is shown in Figure 3.4. But while this is a syntactically correct representation of the equations of an equilibrium model, the causal interpretation is actually that M^s, M^d and i are jointly determined since we cannot assign causal precedence within the loop that connects them. Another way of putting this is to say that the topography of the flowgraph implied by the equations is not unique.

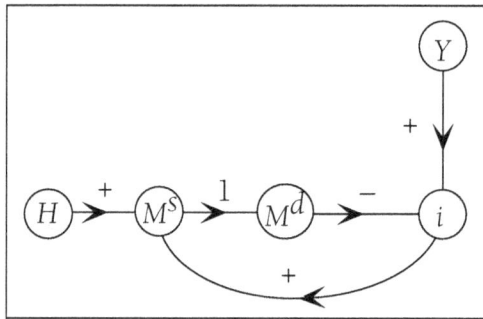

Figure 3.4 LM with interest feedback

However, the qualitative effects of changes in the exogenous variables H and Y are the same as before, e.g. an increase in H reduces i and an increase in Y increases i. And it is still true to say that in order to maintain equilibrium in the money market when there is an increase in high powered money the interest rate has to fall.

Exercise 5

Use equations (1) and (2) to re-express the LM flowgraph of Figure 3.4 with algebraic transmittances, and derive expressions for the effects of (i) a shift in money demand, (ii) a government purchase of treasury bills, (iii) an increase in the price level and (iv) an increase in GDP on the endogenous variables i, m^d and m^s.

3.5 The process of adjustment in the money market

The money market is in equilibrium when the demand for money is equal to the supply of money. But how is this condition brought about? If there is an excess demand for money then people will attempt to acquire the desired amount of money by selling other financial assets, converting them to cash or bank deposits. But of course the money thus acquired by one person is given up by another person. So, overall, nothing appears to have changed. However, the general pressure to sell bonds and other financial assets pushes down their prices, and as the price of bonds falls so the interest rate on bonds rises. This in turn both reduces the demand for money and increases the supply of money. Thus the excess demand for money diminishes, and the process continues until equilibrium is brought about. It has been achieved by changes in the interest rate.

Note that, unlike the equilibrium reasoning of the previous section, this description of the dynamic process of adjustment is inherently causal and is naturally represented as a flowgraph. The model is now written down as an explicitly linear model, albeit linear in the *logarithms* of income, money and the price level, using the equations for money supply and demand set out in equations (1) and (2) above.

$$m^s = m^s_0 + m_1 i + h$$

$$m^d = m^d_0 + \beta_1 y - \beta_2 i + p$$

$$\Delta i = \mu(m^d - m^s)$$

The third equation represents the dynamic adjustment process: the rate of change in the interest rate is proportional to the excess demand for money. The level of the interest rate is the accumulated value of these changes. The flowgraph is shown in Figure 3.5. To avoid clutter it abstracts from the constant terms in the equations. Note that it has a unique topography.

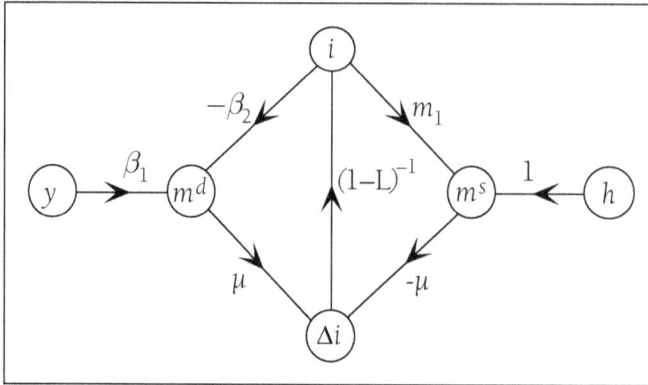

Figure 3.5 Adjustment in the money market

Exercise 6

Using Mason's rule, derive the transmittances from the exogenous variables y and h to the endogenous variables. Infer the long run or steady state effects, and check that they conform with the equilibrium model of Exercise 5.

Is the long-run impact of an increase in y or h on i magnified or attenuated by increased interest sensitivity of the supply of money?

4

The IS-LM Model

4.1 Putting it together

The closed economy IS-LM model combines the IS and LM models set out in chapters 2 and 3, and presented separately again in Figure 4.1.

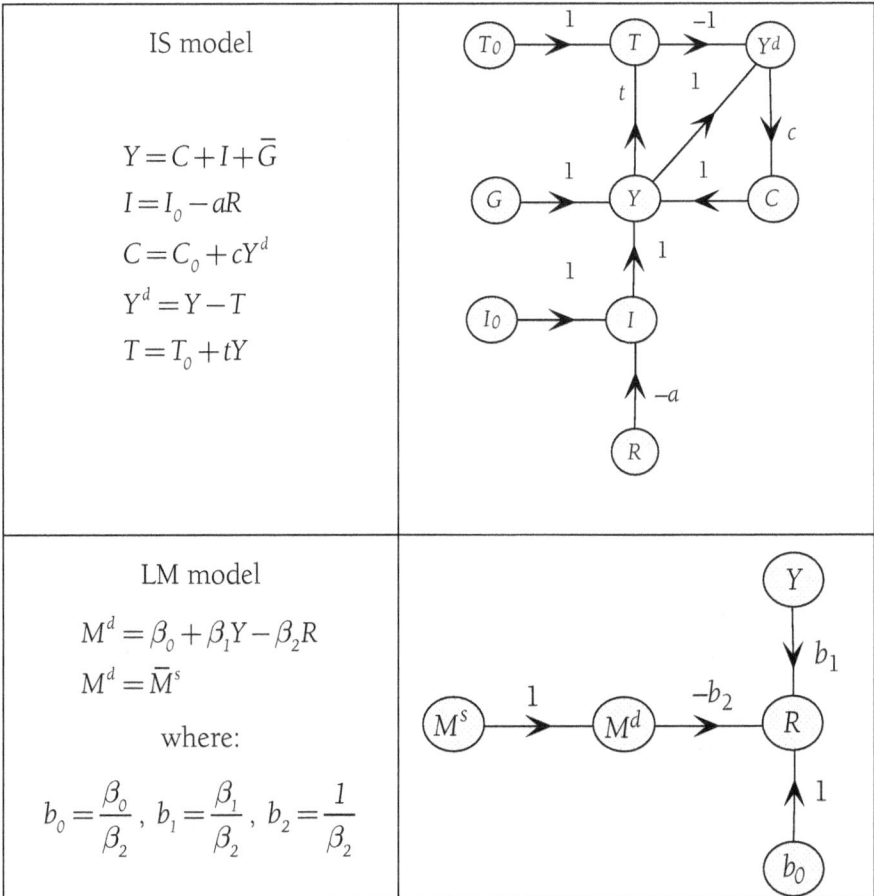

IS model $Y = C + I + \bar{G}$ $I = I_0 - aR$ $C = C_0 + cY^d$ $Y^d = Y - T$ $T = T_0 + tY$	
LM model $M^d = \beta_0 + \beta_1 Y - \beta_2 R$ $M^d = \bar{M}^s$ where: $b_0 = \dfrac{\beta_0}{\beta_2}$, $b_1 = \dfrac{\beta_1}{\beta_2}$, $b_2 = \dfrac{1}{\beta_2}$	

Figure 4.1: IS and LM as separate ingredients

An important point to note is that when the price level is not expected to change, then the real interest rate is equal to the nominal rate, $R = i$. This is what is assumed in chapters 4 to 7. Combining the IS and LM models is straightforwardly accomplished in flowgraph terms by superimposing the two common nodes, Y and R. Note that each of these variables is endogenous in one of the sub-models and exogenous in the other. Both are endogenous in the combined model.

The real goods market and the money market are shown linked together in the IS-LM model presented in Figure 4.2, in which inessential details, *i.e.* certain intermediate variables and shift parameters, are suppressed. The exogenous variables are those nodes which only have outflowing arcs: G, T_0 and M^s. We can use the graph to ask how variations in these exogenous variables affect the endogenous variables which are displayed, namely C, Y and R.

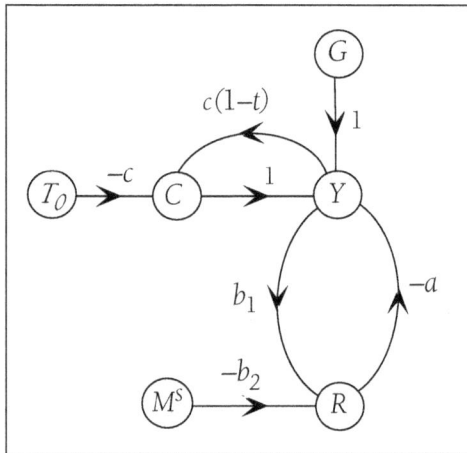

Figure 4.2: The coupled IS-LM system

The IS-LM flowgraph has a rather simple structure, with only two loops and just one direct path from any exogenous variable to any endogenous variable. The two loops touch as they share a common node in Y, and since one loop transmittance is positive but less than one in value, $L_1=c(1-t)$, and the other is negative, $L_2=-ab_1$, it follows that the system determinant $\Delta=1-L_1-L_2$ is positive. But we can deduce the signs of the effects of changes in the exogenous variables without doing algebra, by simply inspecting the signs of the arc transmittances along the paths of the flowgraph. For example, an increase in autonomous taxes T_0, reduces C, which in turn reduces Y and this in turn reduces R.

The flowgraph helps us to avoid crass mistakes, as for example we might make if we consider how a change in money supply affects national income Y. Had we ignored the flowgraph and focussed just on the equations, we might note that Y appears in the money demand function, so it seems that a change in Y can be brought about directly by a change in M^s in the money market equations. But it is evident from the flowgraph that M^s only affects Y through changes in R. This points up the importance of being clear about which variables are exogenous and which endogenous. In the money market Y is exogenous, though it is endogenous in the real product market, and hence also in the IS-LM system as a whole. To make the point starkly, we can see that if investment demand were insensitive to the interest rate (i.e. if $a= 0$), then changes in the money supply could not influence income in this model.

By comparing the IS-LM flowgraph of Figure 4.2 with the simple IS flowgraph of Figure 2.1(b) we can see immediately that the government spending multiplier (i.e. the transmittance from G to Y) must be smaller in the wider IS-LM model because of the extra loop L_2 which increases the denominator in the transmittance but does not affect the numerator. The exact formulae for the transmittances from the exogenous variables to the endogenous variables, can be read directly off the flowgraph by applying Mason's rule. Thus we find:

Exogenous variables	Endogenous variables		
	Y	C	R
T_0	$\dfrac{-c}{\Delta}$	$\dfrac{-c(1+ab_1)}{\Delta}$	$\dfrac{-cb_1}{\Delta}$
G	$\dfrac{1}{\Delta}$	$\dfrac{c(1-t)}{\Delta}$	$\dfrac{b_1}{\Delta}$
M^s	$\dfrac{ab_2}{\Delta}$	$\dfrac{ab_2c(1-t)}{\Delta}$	$\dfrac{-b_2(1-c(1-t))}{\Delta}$
where $\Delta=1+ab_1-c(1-t)$			

Table 4.1 Transmittances in the basic IS-LM model

Note that the entry in the lower right corner of the table, which gives the effect on R of a unit change in M^s, involves a cofactor term in the numerator because of the multiplier loop which does not touch the path concerned. Thus the higher the marginal propensity to consume c, the larger the impact of a change in the money supply on the interest rate, for two reasons: because the numerator rises and because the denominator falls. Similarly the cofactor term in the transmission from T_0 to C implies that the stronger the feedback between the real goods market and money market (the ab_1 term), the lower the impact of autonomous taxes on consumption.

We proceed to examine variations in the specification of the IS-LM model, such as new relations (arcs) or new variables (nodes), changing the routes of paths between nodes, and inverting a path between exogenous and endogenous variables.

Exercise 7

i. Derive some of the transmittances shown in Table 4.1 by the operations of condensing a graph explained in Chapter 1.

ii. Introduce an equation for the money supply, $M^s = M_0 + dR$ giving feedback from the interest rate to the supply of money, and recalculate the transmittances of Table 4.1 (replacing M^s with M_0 as an exogenous variable).

4.2   Dynamics in the IS-LM model

It is usually assumed that the speed of adjustment in the money market is much faster than that in the real product market, so that for many purposes it is appropriate to consider the money market to be more or less continuously in equilibrium. Then we only need to consider dynamic adjustment in the IS sector of the model. A simple dynamic process that is consistent with the usual explanation of adjustment in the final product market can be introduced by replacing the equality between income and output in the model with an equation in which a difference between final expenditure E (= $C + I + G$) and output Y induces a change in output:

$$\Delta Y = (1-L)Y = \lambda L(E-Y).$$

Here the positive coefficient λ represents the speed of adjustment. A value of λ equal to one corresponds to the earlier model of IS dynamics in Section 2.2. Note that the difference between expenditure and output is inventory accumulation or stockbuilding. Now our flowgraph of the system can be represented as in Figure 4.3.

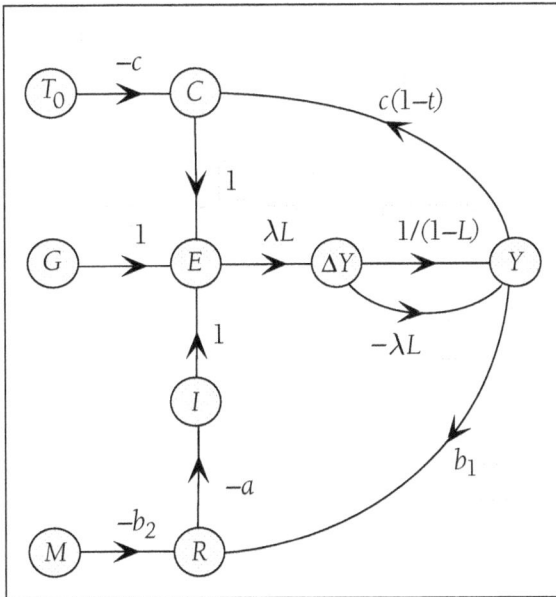

Figure 4.3 Dynamic adjustment in IS sector

The system determinant is:

$$\Delta = 1 + \frac{\lambda L}{1-L} - \frac{\lambda Lc(1-t)}{1-L} + \frac{\lambda Lb_1 a}{1-L}$$

and the transmittance:

$$\left\langle \frac{Y}{G} \right\rangle = \frac{\lambda L/(1-L)}{1 + \lambda L(1-c(1-t)+b_1 a)/(1-L)} = \frac{\lambda L}{1-L+\lambda L(1-c(1-t)+b_1 a)}$$

To find the equilibrium effect of a change in G on Y, set the lag operator L equal to 1. This yields the long-run or steady state effect and gives the same result for the transmittance from G to Y as that shown in Table 4.1, confirming that our static model is the equilibrium outcome of this dynamic formulation of the IS-LM model.

4.3   Can tax cuts be deflationary?

Applied econometricians often experiment with the specification of individual relationships in a model. The demand for money is a prime example. Money may be broad or narrow; interest rates may be long or short; the "scale" variable representing the volume of transactions may be GDP, permanent income or consumers' expenditure. We consider just the scale variable, and follow Mankiw and Summers[†] in specifying it to be consumer spending instead of GDP. This apparently innocuous change to the IS-LM model is actually highly significant, as can be easily seen if we work with a flowgraph representation, shown in Figure 4.4.

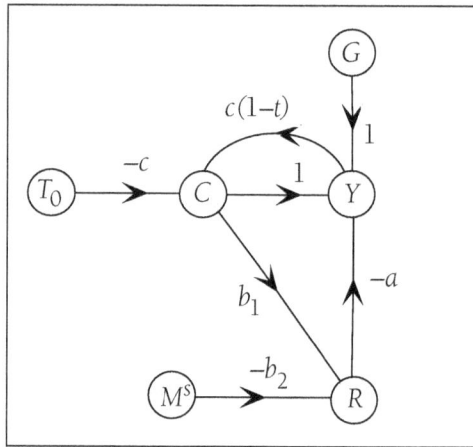

Figure 4.4: Consumption as the "scale variable"

Now there are two direct paths from the level of autonomous taxes (or tax allowances) to GDP. Both paths go through consumption, but the new route is a path from consumption via the rate of interest to GDP. The new path has a positive transmittance $T_2 = cb_1a$, because an increase in taxes reduces consumption, which reduces the interest rate which stimulates investment and GDP. So this path offsets the negative transmittance along the "normal" path $T_1 = -c$, giving rise to the counter-intuitive possibility of "deflationary tax cuts", first noted by Holmes and Smyth[‡]. By Mason's rule the transmittance from tax to GDP is:

[†] N. G. Mankiw and L. Summers, "Money demand and the effects of fiscal policies", *Journal of Money, Credit and Banking*, 1986, vol. 18, pp. 415 - 429.
[‡] J. Holmes and D. Smyth, "The specification of the demand for money and the tax multiplier", *Journal of Political Economy*, 1972, vol. 80, pp. 179-185.

$$\left(\frac{Y}{T_0}\right)=\frac{c(ab_1-1)}{1-c(1-t)+ab_1c(1-t)}=\frac{?}{+}$$

The critical condition is the sign of the term in brackets in the numerator. The flowgraph gives a clear and immediate explanation of the curiosum. However, note that it does not survive in a model that takes account of the Government's budget constraint (see Exercise 8 below).

4.4 Reversal of causality: the interest rate as an instrument of policy

If the monetary authority sets the interest rate, *i.e.* makes it exogenous, then the money supply becomes endogenous. Consider the IS-LM model of Figure 4.2 which is redrawn in a simplified form in Figure 4.5(a) by absorbing endogenous nodes or omitting exogenous nodes which are irrelevant to our purpose. Note that the new composite parameters are defined as $\alpha=a/(1-c(1-t))$ and $\gamma=1/(1-c(1-t))$. The causality-reversed model is shown in Figure 4.5 (b). Note that whereas the original graph contains a loop, the new graph comprises only direct paths.

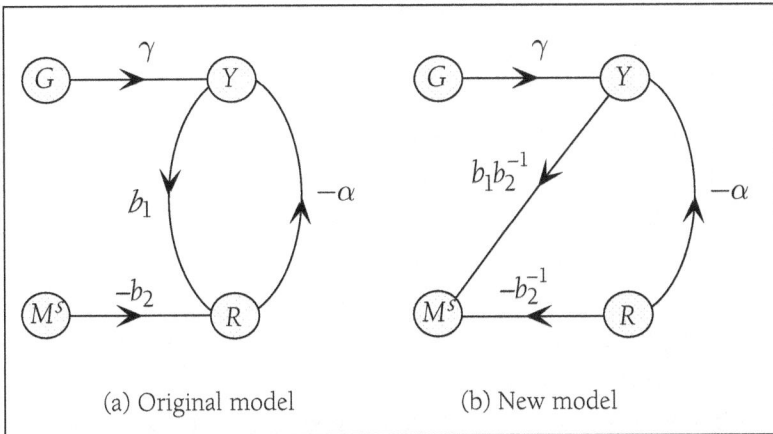

(a) Original model   (b) New model

Figure 4.5: Reversal of causality in the IS-LM model

The method for "inverting a path", or reversing causality, was explained in Chapter 1. It is worth noting that in the new model the feedback loop between the money market and the real product market has disappeared, and with R exogenous, there are two paths by which a change in the rate of interest affects the now endogenous money supply. An increase in the interest rate has a direct negative effect via the demand for money, and in addition it reduces income, which also reduces the demand for money. It is also worth noting that government spending now has a stronger effect on income than before because of the absence of a feedback loop between the real and monetary sectors, which implies no financial crowding out of investment. In this model the transmittance is $\gamma = 1/(1-c(1-t))$, whereas formerly it was $1/(1-c(1-t)+ab_1)$.

4.5   IS-LM with a balanced budget

Often, the textbook IS-LM model is presented as in the earlier sections of this chapter, paying no attention to the government's budget constraint. The simplest assumption that respects the budget constraint is that the government balances its budget—i.e. matches revenue and spending. This adds an eighth equation to those set out in Figure 4.1:

$$T = G.$$

If we adhere to the earlier assumption that G is exogenous, then the balanced budget must determine total taxes T, and this makes the fixed component of taxes, T_0 endogenous. Thus "autonomous" taxes and tax allowances are adjusted to maintain the equality between government expenditures and revenues. This gives the flowgraphs shown in Figure 4.6, which differ with respect to the scale variable in the demand for money function, continuing the earlier theme.

The flowgraphs in Figure 4.6 could be simplified by eliminating the T and T_0 nodes, but displaying the tax detail clarifies their connection with the equations, and shows the new arc from G to T, and the consequent endogenization of T_0. It is interesting to compare the budget multipliers in these two models by applying Mason's rule to the two flowgraphs. They are recorded in Table 4.2.

Note the surprisingly stark implications of Model (b) in which consumer spending is the scale variable in the demand for money. All these

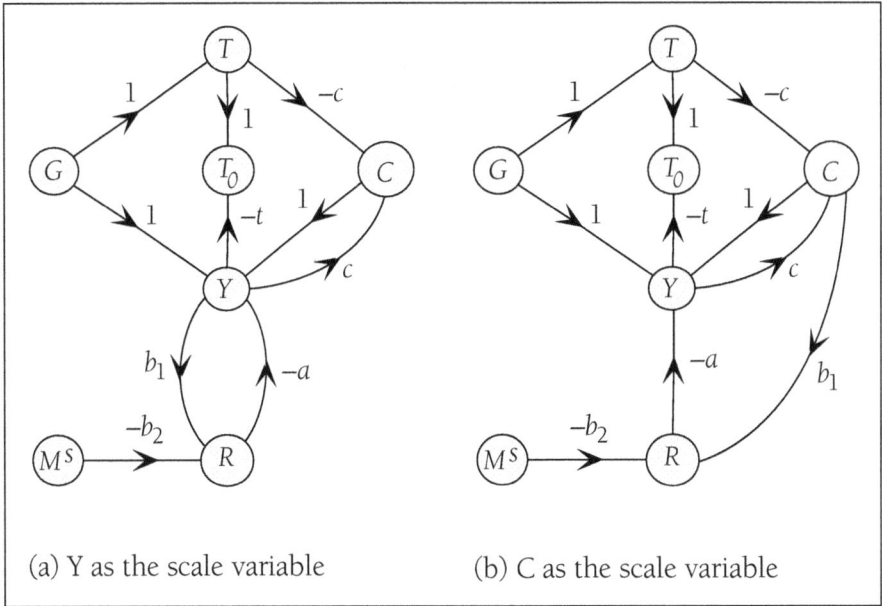

(a) Y as the scale variable   (b) C as the scale variable

Figure 4.6: IS-LM models with balanced budgets

	Model	
Effect of $\Delta G = 1$ on:	(a)	(b)
Y	$\dfrac{1-c}{1-c+ab_1}$	1
C	$\dfrac{-cab_1}{1-c+ab_1}$	0
R	$\dfrac{b_1(1-c)}{1-c+ab_1}$	0

Table 4.2 Transmittances in two versions of the balanced budget IS-LM model

transmittances can be written down virtually on inspection of the flow-graphs, and the flowgraphs also support explanation. For example, consider the difference between the GDP multipliers in the two models. The larger multiplier in model (b) is explained by the extra path via the rate of interest. To account for the multiplier being exactly one in model (b), note that G can have no effect on C because of the two exactly offsetting paths, and therefore it can have no effect on I (not shown explicitly, but located between R and Y) because all paths from G to I go through C. Since Y is the sum of these components, changes in G must induce equal changes in Y.

Exercise 8

Modify the flowgraphs of Figure 4.6 to make the level of autonomous taxes T_0 exogenous and G endogenous. Now compare the transmittance from T_0 to Y in the two models, and establish whether deflationary tax cuts are possible in the model which has consumption as the scale variable in the money demand function.

4.6 IS-LM model with monetized deficits

Earlier, in Section 4.2, we considered dynamics in the IS-LM model arising from a process of adjustment between equilibria. By contrast, we now consider a variation on the IS-LM model in which the dynamic process is an essential feature of the equilibrium itself. Now the government budget constraint is modified to allow an unbalanced budget, in which deficits are financed by printing money, and so add to the monetary base. The model thus includes the seven equations of Figure 4.1, which are combined in the following two equations:

$$Y_t = Y_0 - a_1 R_t + a_2 G_t - c a_2 T_{0t} \tag{1}$$

$$R_t = b_0 + b_1 Y_t - b_2 M_t \tag{2}$$

where the parameters of (1), expressed in terms of the notation of Section 4.1 are:

$$Y_0 = \frac{C_0 + I_0}{1 - c(1-t)}, \quad a_1 = \frac{a}{1 - c(1-t)} \quad \text{and} \quad a_2 = \frac{1}{1 - c(1-t)}.$$

To these we add three equations which represent the effect of the budget on the money supply:

$$D_t = G_t - T_t \tag{3}$$

$$H_t = H_{t-1} + D_{t-1} \tag{4}$$

$$M_t^s = m H_t \tag{5}$$

where D is the government deficit (a flow), H is the stock of high-powered money (monetary base) and m is the money multiplier. The mixture of stocks and flows requires us to date the variables with subscripts and to be explicit about the point in time that stocks are measured. Here the money stocks are assumed to be measured at the *beginning* of the period. It now simplifies matters to remove the time subscripts and use the lag operator L instead. In this notation equation (4) becomes:

$$H = LH + LD \qquad\qquad (4a)$$

Recall that in IS-LM models the price level is assumed to be fixed, but note that this assumption would not be plausible if the deficits produced a sustained expansion of the money supply. A flowgraph representation is given in Figure 4.7.

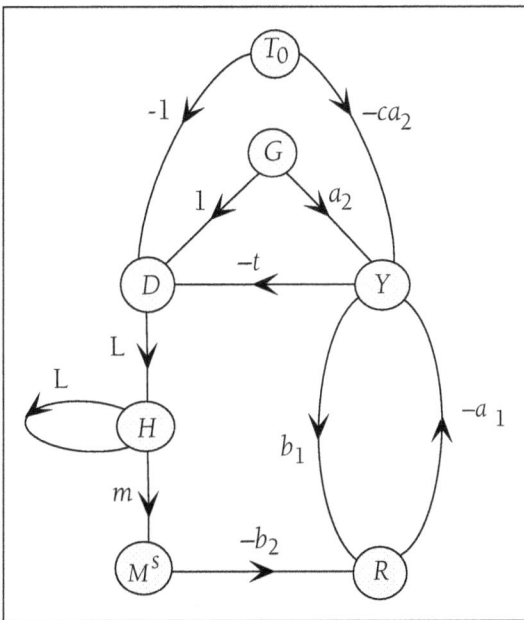

Figure 4.7: Monetised deficits

The transmittance of the self-loop on H is simply the lag operator, L. It is the main dynamic element in this model. It implies that H is changing as long as there is any input into that node, *i.e.* whenever the deficit D is non-zero. This is what accounts for change and equilibrium in the model.

Let us examine how variations in the exogenous variable G affect Y. There are three loops, with path transmittances, $L_1=-a_1b_1$, $L_2=-mb_2a_1tL$, and $L_3=L$. Loops L_1 and L_3 do not touch, so the system determinant is

$$\Delta(L)=1-L+a_1b_1+mb_2a_1tL-a_1b_1L,$$

where the last term is the product of the non-touching loops. There are two paths from G to Y, and Mason's rule gives the overall transmittance as:

$$\left\langle\frac{Y}{G}\right\rangle=\frac{a_2(1-L)+mb_2a_1L}{\Delta(L)}$$

This formula gives the complete response of Y to any assumed time path of G as a difference equation. However, the short- and long-run responses to a step increase in G are usually of greatest interest. They are derived by setting L to zero and one respectively.

Short-run multiplier: $\left\langle\dfrac{Y}{G}\right\rangle \xrightarrow{\ L=0\ } \dfrac{a_2}{1+a_1b_1}$

Now, translating the parameters a_1 and a_2 into the combinations of more basic parameters noted above, we find:

$$\left\langle\frac{Y}{G}\right\rangle \xrightarrow{\ L=0\ } \frac{1}{1-c(1-t)+ab_1}\,,$$

which is the basic government spending multiplier in the static IS-LM model.

Long-run multiplier: $\left\langle\dfrac{Y}{G}\right\rangle \xrightarrow{\ L=1\ } \dfrac{mb_2a_1}{mb_2a_1t}=\dfrac{1}{t}$

Thus the long-run multiplier is the inverse of the marginal rate of income tax.

An explanation of these results in terms of the flowgraph is that there are two channels (paths) for an increase in government spending to influence GDP: the direct channel and an indirect channel via the money market. The indirect path working through the money supply gradually amplifies the expansionary effect of government spending. Compare this with the case in which the budget is always balanced, shown in Figure 4.6(a), where a second indirect path has negative transmittance, offsetting the directly expansionary effect of an increase in G.

Of crucial importance in the present dynamic model is the self-loop on H. It can be consolidated into the arc that leads into H, which then becomes $(1-L)^{-1}$ which goes to infinity as L goes to one in the long-run case. The only paths (and path cofactors) that matter in the long run are those that include this component, which dominates all other paths.

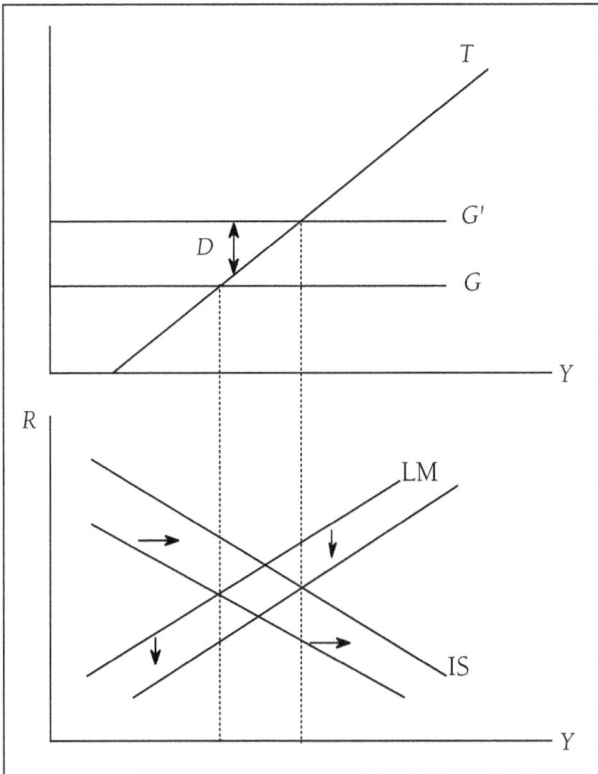

Figure 4.8 Standard IS-LM representation

The standard IS-LM representation of this model is shown in Figure 4.8. In the very short run the change in government spending directly affects both the deficit D and aggregate demand Y. The IS curve shifts once for all to the right and output increases, as does the interest rate.

Over time the increased deficit accumulates into an expansion of high powered money which makes the LM curve move gradually downwards, expanding output still further but bringing the interest rate back down. The LM curve continues to move downwards while there is a deficit to be financed by expanding the money stock, and this goes on until sufficient extra taxes are generated from the increased output to bring the deficit to zero. Thus equilibrium is eventually restored. Hence the long-run aggregate demand multiplier for this model can be inferred from the upper diagram, bearing in mind that the slope of tax function is t. However, the eventual effect on the interest rate is ambiguous. It rises in the long-run if $a > 1 - c(1-t)$, as can be verified by solving for the long-run transmittance from G to R.

5

Open Economy
with a Fixed Exchange Rate

Up to this point we have ignored interactions between economies, considering our economy to be closed and entirely self-sufficient, *i.e.* an "autarky". This might be appropriate for the economy of the whole world. But also some countries have been near autarkies, either because of their physical circumstances, *e.g.* Hawaii and Nepal in the past, or through political choice, *e.g.* Burma (Myanmar) in these days, Albania in the Communist era, Spain and Portugal between 1939 and 1959. However, most economies interact; that is to say they influence and are themselves influenced by other economies, either through trade in goods and services, or through capital transactions with residents of other countries.

Throughout this chapter it is assumed that the exchange rate is fixed and unchanging. The case of flexible exchange rates will be considered in Chapter 6. Here, in Section 5.1 we consider economies that are only open in the sense that they trade goods and services with the rest of the world. We develop a static model by adding a foreign trade sector to the closed economy IS-LM model. For short-run effects this is a minor change, but trade imbalances lead to the accumulation or decumulation of domestically held stocks of foreign currency, and so have dynamic consequences. This can be analysed in a static model by recognising that such accumulations are not sustainable indefinitely, so that in the long run trade will balance. Then incorporating an exogenous zero trade balance into the model yields the long-run of the model. An alternative treatment which explicitly models the dynamics of this model is presented in Section 5.2. The concept of openness is widened in the remainder of the chapter by removing the assumption that capital is immobile between countries. A simple asymmetric two-country model with perfect capital mobility is presented in Section 5.3 and a more general dynamic model which assumes capital to be imperfectly mobile is presented in Section 5.4. Finally, a model of perfect capital mobility is presented in Section 5.5 as a limiting case of imperfect capital mobility, and shown to be congruent with a static model of an autarky.

5.1   Immobile capital: static model

Here we consider economies that are only open in the sense that they trade goods and services with the rest of the world. We develop the static model by adding a foreign trade sector to the closed economy IS-LM model. Although trade imbalances lead to the accumulation or decumulation of domestically held stocks of foreign currency, which has dynamic consequences, the model is kept static by specifying two separate models, one for the short run and one for the long run. The long-run model is derived from the short-run model by recognizing that the long run corresponds to a situation in which there is a zero balance of trade, with imports exactly matching exports. Since there are no capital movements between countries, the balance of trade is identical with the balance of payments. In the short run the balance of trade is endogenous, but in the long run it is constrained to be zero, and therefore becomes exogenous. Thus the flowgraph of the long-run static model can be derived from the flowgraph of the short-run static model by reversing causality and exogenizing the balance of trade. To do this we need to specify which short-run exogenous variable is to become endogenous. The natural candidate for this is the money stock, and this is consistent with the explicit dynamic analysis of Section 5.2.

The trade balance, or net exports B, is the difference between exports and imports:

$$B = X - Z = X - zY$$

where X is exports, usually treated as exogenous, and Z is imports, which increase with the level of output in the economy. The parameter z

is the marginal propensity to import. The income-expenditure equation is now:

$$Y = C + I + G + B$$

By incorporating these modifications to the IS-LM model of Chapter 4 we arrive at the model displayed in Figure 5.1.

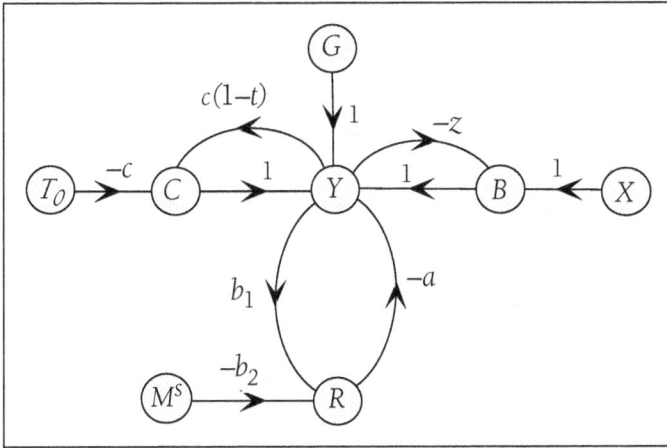

Figure 5.1: The IS-LM model with trade

The effect of foreign trade is to attenuate all the expenditure multipliers in the system because the balance of trade loop introduces an extra term into the denominators. Thus the government spending multiplier—the transmittance from G to Y—becomes

$$\left\langle \frac{Y}{G} \right\rangle = \frac{1}{1 - c(1-t) + ab_1 + z}$$

in which the last term in the denominator arises from the "leakage" due to imports. The export multiplier is identical to the government spending multiplier. However, the addition of foreign trade to the model increases the sensitivity of the interest rate to changes in the stock of money since the transmittance is now:

$$\left\langle \frac{R}{M} \right\rangle = \frac{-b_2(1 - c(1-t) + z)}{1 - c(1-t) + ab_1 + z}$$

which differs from the closed economy transmittance in having the z terms in both numerator and denominator. They have the effect of increasing the absolute value of the transmittance—the partial derivative of the transmittance with respect to z is negative, so the larger is z the further R falls for a given increase in M. Despite this, the effect of a change in the money supply on Y is less than in the autarky (*i.e.* no trade) model.

We now consider the difference between the short run and the long run. The long run is a situation in which the trade balance is zero. So in the long run we consider B to be exogenous. This change endogenizes the money supply, M^s. Thus causality reversal, or path inversion, is involved. To illustrate this, the flowgraph of Figure 5.1 is first simplified by absorbing the C node and collecting all autonomous components of expenditure into the term $A = G - cT_0 + C_0 + I_0$. Absorbing the C node eliminates the C–Y loop, whose effects are incorporated in the arc transmittances of all arcs leading into Y. Thus in Figure 5.2(i) the parameters a_1 and a_2 are a composites of the model parameters, with:

$$a_1 = \frac{a}{1-c(1-t)}, \text{ and } a_2 = \frac{1}{1-c(1-t)}.$$

The layout of the flowgraph in Figure 5.2(i) was chosen with the path-inverted flowgraph 5.2(ii) in mind, to avoid intersecting arcs and to keep the nodes in similar positions. Path inversion is a reversible operation, so one can go back and forth between the short-run and the long-run flowgraphs.

In the *short run* an increase in exports increases the trade balance B, which leads to an increase in output Y and an increased interest rate R. By comparison, an increase in autonomous expenditure A leads to the same increases in Y and R, but reduces the trade balance. In the *long run* the trade balance is exogenous; an increase in exports also increases income in the long run, though the degree to which it does so is now inversely proportional to the marginal propensity to import z, because imports must rise sufficiently to exactly match the increased exports. An increase in autonomous expenditure has no effect on output in the long run, but pushes up the interest rate. This occurs because output must be maintained constant so as to maintain imports constant (with given X), so if autonomous components of aggregate demand have risen, that rise must be offset by a decline in the interest-sensitive components of aggregate demand.

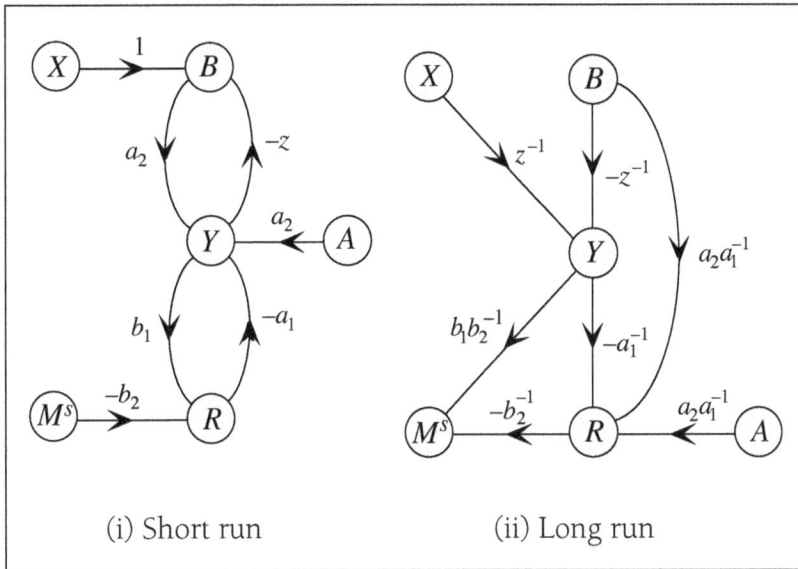

Figure 5.2: Short-run and long-run with trade balance

Exercise 9

i.   Explain the attenuation of expenditure multipliers in the short-run model in terms of a Keynesian cross diagram.

ii. Compare the long- and short-run effects of increases in X and G on R.

iii. Reverse the causality from Ms to B in Figure 5.2(ii) to recover Figure 5.2(i).

iv. Explain the long-run effects of X and G on Y and R in terms of an IS-LM diagram.

5.2 Immobile capital: dynamic model

Capital immobility characterized the situation in much of Europe in the 1950s and 1960s, and still holds in parts of the developing world today: foreigners are prevented from investing in the economy, and domestic residents are prevented from investing abroad. So capital flows are eliminated. We must now be explicit about how the exchange rate is kept fixed. This is achieved by adjustment of the central bank's reserves of foreign currency. The bank buys foreign currency when there is a current account surplus, and sells foreign currency when there is a current account deficit, exactly matching the current account balance B by a change in the bank's stock of foreign exchange reserves F. The stock of high-powered money H is the sum of central bank reserves of foreign currency and the outstanding stock of government securities held by the commercial banks, S. The equations of the model are:

$$Y = -a_1 R + a_2 (A + B) \tag{1}$$

$$R = R_0 + b_1 Y - b_2 M \tag{2}$$

$$B = -zY + X \tag{3}$$

$$F = LF + LB \tag{4}$$

$$H = F + S \tag{5}$$

$$M = mH \tag{6}$$

where A is autonomous spending, which includes government expenditure, B is the balance of trade, X is exports, zY is imports and L is the lag operator. Equation (1) states that total expenditure is the sum of a component that is induced by the interest rate and a component comprising the sum of the trade balance and autonomous spending. Fiscal changes are included within A. Thus equation (1) is a reduced form summary of the income-expenditure system which corresponds to the IS curve, and equation (2) corresponds to the LM curve. Equation (3) states that the balance of trade is exports less imports. Equation (4) states that foreign currency reserves at the *beginning* of the current period are the sum of reserves at the beginning of the previous period and last period's trade balance. Note that all stocks are measured at the beginning of the period. Equation (5) defines the stock of "high powered" money as the sum of foreign exchange reserves held by the central bank and government securities held by banks. Equation (6) gives the stock of money as a multiple of high-powered money.

The causal representation of the model is shown in Figure 5.3.

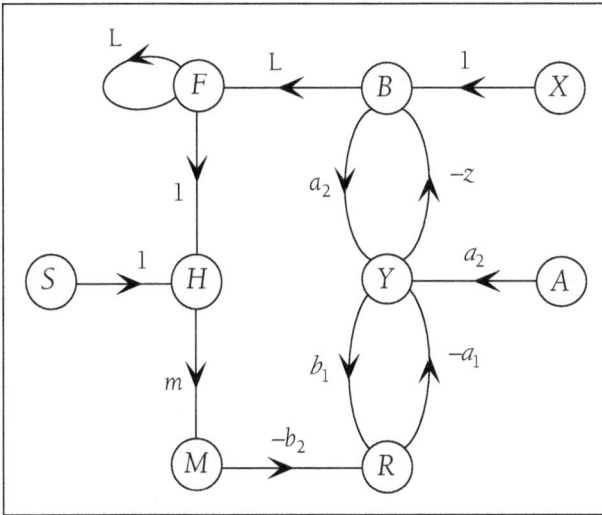

Figure 5.3: Open to trade, but not to capital flows

The short- and long-run effects of the exogenous variables S, A, and X on any of the endogenous variables can be ascertained directly from the flowgraph. Thus, in the short-run we can infer the following effects. An increase in exports increases the trade balance, output and the interest rate, but it has no effect on the money stocks H and M because of the lag (set $L=0$). A positive shock to domestic demand (an increase in A) increases GDP and the interest rate, but decreases the trade balance due to increased import demand; it too has no immediate effect on the money stocks. Increased holdings of government securities by the banks are represented by an increase in S, which increases the stock of money, reduces the interest rate and thereby increases output Y and reduces the trade balance B due to higher imports. Note that the loops which do not include L both have negative loop transmittance, so the system determinant is assuredly positive, and the signs of transmittances are the same as the signs of the direct paths.

In the long run we only consider paths that include the F node because of the dominating effect of the self-loop as $L \rightarrow 1$. Thus in the long run an increase in S has no effect on any variable other than F, which must fall by a compensating amount in order to keep H unchanged. An increase in A, such as increased government spending, has no effect on Y or B, but reduces F, H and M and thereby increases R. Thus private spending is crowded out. An increase in X increases reserves F and the money stocks H and M. It thereby decreases R and increases Y.

For the algebraic transmittances it is useful to factorize the system determinant into two parts, containing terms involving L and (1–L) for the short run and the long run respectively:

$$\Delta = (1-L)(1+a_2z+a_1b_1) + mb_2a_1zL \ .$$

Then if the numerator for any transmittance is similarly factorized into terms involving 1–L and L and other terms, the implications of L going to zero or one are immediately apparent.

Exogenous variables	Endogenous variables	
	Y	R
A	$\dfrac{a_2(1-L)}{\Delta}$	$\dfrac{a_2b_1(1-L)+a_2zmb_2L}{\Delta}$
X	$\dfrac{a_2(1-L)+mb_2a_1L}{\Delta}$	$\dfrac{a_2b_1(1-L)-mb_2L}{\Delta}$
S	$\dfrac{mb_2a_1(1-L)}{\Delta}$	$\dfrac{-mb_2(1-L+a_2z-a_2zL)}{\Delta}$
where $\Delta = (1-L)(1+a_2z+a_1b_1)+mb_2a_1zL$		

Table 5.1a Transmittances in the open economy without capital flows

Exogenous variables	Endogenous variables	
	Y	R
A	$\dfrac{a_2}{\Delta(0)}$	$\dfrac{a_2b_1}{\Delta(0)}$
X	$\dfrac{a_2}{\Delta(0)}$	$\dfrac{a_2b_1}{\Delta(0)}$
S	$\dfrac{mb_2a_1}{\Delta(0)}$	$\dfrac{-mb_2(1+a_2z)}{\Delta(0)}$
where $\Delta(0)=1+a_2z+a_1b_1$		

Table 5.1b Short-run (impact) effects in the open economy without capital flows

The algebraic summary of Table 5.1a confirms the qualitative inferences above. Note that the impact effect on income of a step change in autonomous spending is the same as that of a step change in exports, yet in the long run autonomous spending has no effect on income but exports have a powerful multiplier, which is the inverse of the marginal propensity to import, z.

Exogenous variables	Endogenous variables	
	Y	R
A	0	$\dfrac{a_2}{a_1}$
X	$\dfrac{1}{z}$	$-\dfrac{1}{a_1 z}$
S	0	0

Table 5.1c Long-run effects in the open economy without capital flows

For a "reality check", note that this model gives a plausible characterization of the experiences of West Germany and the U.K. in the 1950s and 1960s. West Germany's sustained "economic miracle" was fueled by export demand, whereas the U.K.'s experience was to discover the counterproductive consequences of increases in domestic spending as an unsustainable stimulus to GDP.

Translating between the flowgraph of Figure 5.3 and an explanation in terms of the usual IS-LM diagram, note that the path from R to Y corresponds to the IS curve. It is shifted rightwards (Y increases for given R) by an increase in A or X. The path that goes from Y to R without passing F corresponds to the instantaneous LM curve. It is shifted instantaneously by changes in S. But it is also shifted gradually as F accumulates or runs down over time, which occurs so long as B is not zero. Thus an increase in A, for example a fiscal expansion, immediately shifts the IS curve rightwards, but because it also induces a negative balance of trade, this causes the LM curve to move gradually upwards. The gradual movement of the LM curve only terminates when B is zero, which must be at the original level of output Y because imports equal the unchanged exports at that output. The process is illustrated in Figure 5.4, in which the original equilibrium is at I, the fiscal expansion takes the economy to II in the short term, but the gradual shift of the LM curve upwards due to the decline in money brought about by the trade deficit only stops when Y is returned to its original level at III, with the interest rate raised.

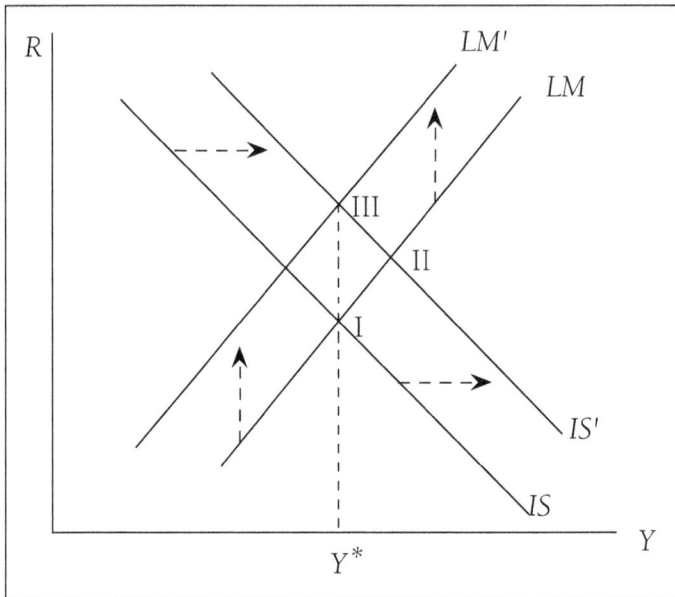

Figure 5.4: Fiscal expansion and gradual adjustment

Explanations for some long-run implications of the model are rather subtle if we work within a long-run comparative static framework. Take for example the logic of an increase in exports reducing the interest rate in the long run. The argument is that in the long run the balance of trade B balances; i.e. it is exogenous and equal to zero. Consequently an increase in exports must be matched by an equal increase in imports, which requires an increase in expenditure Y, with a multiplier equal to the inverse of the marginal propensity to import. Since A and B are exogenous, the required increase in expenditure can only be brought about by an increase in the interest-sensitive components of expenditure, which requires a reduction in the interest rate. The equations of the model provide an effective chain of reasoning by backward induction. Thus the long run corresponds to a value of 1 for the lag operator L, which from equation (4) implies that $B=0$. Hence, from (3) we infer that $Y=X/z$, and so on. The chain of reasoning, given that X and A are exogenous is illustrated as follows:

$$L=1 \xrightarrow{4} B=0 \xrightarrow{3} Y=X/z \xrightarrow{1} R=(-Y+a_2(A+B))/a_1$$
$$\xrightarrow{2} M=(R+b_1Y)/b_2 \xrightarrow{6} H=M/m \xrightarrow{5} F=H-S$$

where a number over an implication arrow signals the equation that delivers that implication. This is equivalent to the causal flowgraph shown in Figure 5.5, which can also be derived from Figure 5.3 by inverting the long path from B to F. In this flowgraph, the arcs emanating from the B node would also apply if there were a non-zero target for the balance of trade, but in the present context the B node could simply be ignored.

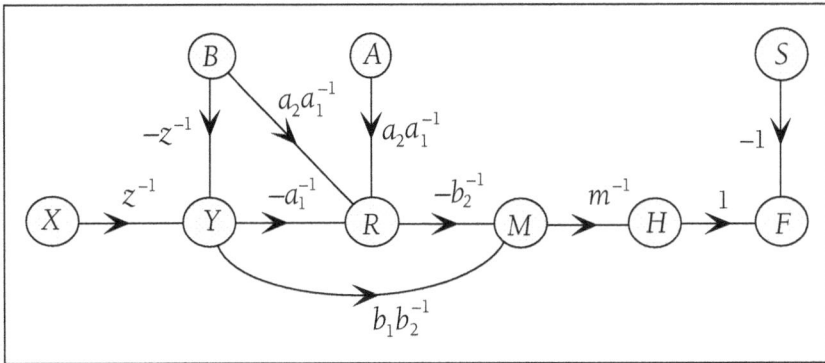

Figure 5.5 Long-run of the balance of trade model

Exercise 10
Give an IS-LM type diagrammatic explanation of the long-run effect of an increase in (a) exports and (b) the money supply in this model.

5.3 Perfect capital mobility

Thus far we have considered models in which the exchange rate is fixed and the balance of payments consists solely of the balance of trade.

Models in which the capital account of the balance of payments plays a role have very different implications. They are also particularly relevant to the modern world of the advanced countries where controls on capital flows have largely disappeared. The low cost of moving portfolio capital between countries suggests an almost perfect mobility of capital between countries. That is to say, portfolio investors can choose to hold bonds and other paper assets where they earn the greatest return. If the exchange rate is fixed, then small differences in interest rates induce large flows of capital in response, so much so that for small countries the effect swamps the domestic demand and supply of bonds, and results in the country having the same interest rate as abroad. Hence an assumption of perfect capital mobility corresponds to an exogenous interest rate for a small country. This of course means that the country's money supply becomes endogenous.

Maintaining the assumption of a fixed exchange rate, we explore a two country model with perfect capital mobility. In this model there is an asymmetry between the countries in that one of them is able to control its money supply or interest rate, whereas the other country takes that interest rate as given exogenously. This set-up may reflect the fact that the economies are of different size, like the U.K. and Ireland when their currencies exchanged one for one in the 1970s, or like Germany and its smaller EC neighbours in the era of the European Monetary System. In the latter case there was also the fact that its track record conferred on the Bundesbank a credibility advantage over other European central banks, which allowed it much autonomy in setting domestic monetary conditions in Germany, to which other economies in the EMS had to adapt.

The equations of the model are as follows:

$$Y = -a_1 R + a_2 A + a_3 Y^* \qquad (1)$$

$$R = b_1 Y - b_2 M \qquad (2)$$

$$R = R^* \qquad (3)$$

$$Y^* = -a_1^* R^* + a_2^* A^* + a_3^* Y \qquad (4)$$

$$R^* = b_1^* Y^* - b_2^* M^*$$ (5)

where equations (1) to (3) determine Y, M and R respectively in the "small" home country, say Belgium, and equations (4) and (5) determine Y^* and R^* in the "large" foreign country, say Germany. Variables and parameters with asterisks pertain to Germany. Equations (1) and (4) represent the IS sector in the two countries, where the final term on the right is exports to the other country. These equations determine output in the relevant country. Equations (2) and (5) represent the LM sectors in the two countries. Equation (5) determines the interest rate in Germany which, from (3), is also adopted in Belgium. Equation (2) determines the stock of money in Belgium. The flowgraph is given in Figure 5.6.

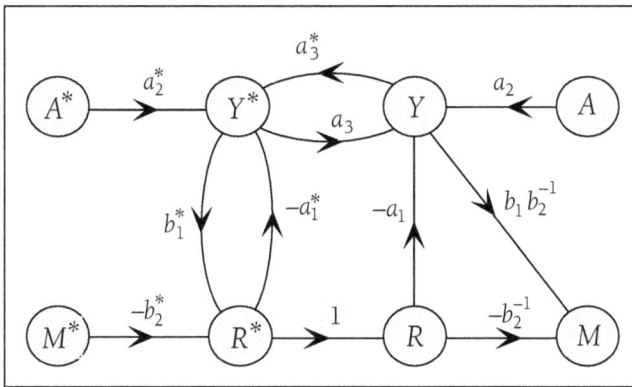

Figure 5.6: Two country IS-LM model

Before discussing detailed formulae, let us qualitatively examine the effects of German financial "hegemony" according to this model, by tracing them through the arcs of the flowgraph. First notice that Germany controls two policy variables, money M^* and fiscal variables in A^*, whereas Belgium has just fiscal policy in A since its money is endogenous. Variations in German money supply affect output in both countries by two routes. In Germany output is affected directly by the change in the interest rate, and indirectly through the effect of the interest rate on Belgian output, and hence German exports to Belgium. Similarly, Belgian output is affected both by the change in the interest rate and by the change in German output which affects Belgian exports to Germany. Looking at the parameters along these paths, a_3 and a_3^*, being the marginal propensities to import in the two countries, are likely to be of similar magnitude. But a_1 is likely to be smaller than a_1^* since these parameters represent the effect of a unit change in the interest rate on output, and by assumption German output is larger than Belgian output.

Turning to fiscal policy, modeled as variations in A or A^*, we find that Belgian fiscal policy is more effective than German fiscal policy since it is not attenuated by direct feedback from the financial sector (the Belgian LM curve is horizontal). Also we see that a Belgian fiscal expansion surely raises German output, but a German fiscal expansion could lower Belgian output! This occurs because while there is just one path from Belgian fiscal policy to German output, via German net exports, there are two offsetting paths from German fiscal policy to Belgian output: in addition to an effect on Belgian net exports, the German fiscal expansion increases the demand for money in Germany and pushes up the interest rate, thus depressing Belgian output.

Exogenous variables	Endogenous variables		
	$R=R^*$	Y^*	Y
M^*	$\dfrac{-b_2^*(1-a_3 a_3^*)}{\Delta}$	$\dfrac{b_2^*(a_1^* + a_1 a_3^*)}{\Delta}$	$\dfrac{b_2^*(a_1 + a_1^* a_3)}{\Delta}$
A^*	$\dfrac{a_2^* b_1^*}{\Delta}$	$\dfrac{a_2^*}{\Delta}$	$\dfrac{a_2^*(a_3 - b_1^* a_1)}{\Delta}$
A	$\dfrac{a_2 a_3^* b_1^*}{\Delta}$	$\dfrac{a_2 a_3^*}{\Delta}$	$\dfrac{a_2(1 + b_1^* a_1^*)}{\Delta}$
where $\Delta = 1 + a_1^* b_1^* + a_1 a_3^* b_1^* - a_3 a_3^*$.			

Table 5.2 Transmittances in the two-country model

The system determinant for the transmittances shown in Table 5.2 is based on the three touching loops: $L_1 = a_3 a_3^*$, $L_2 = -a_1^* b_1^*$ and $L_3 = -a_1 a_3^* b_1^*$, which yield $\Delta = 1 + a_1^* b_1^* + a_1 a_3^* b_1^* - a_3 a_3^*$.

Exercise 11

Construct a linked IS-LM diagram for the two countries and check its qualitative implications with those of Table 5.2.

5.4 Imperfect capital mobility

The combination of mobile capital with a fixed exchange rate broadly characterized the normal situation in most of the European Community in the 1980s and the 1990s under the European exchange rate mechanism, in which exchange parities between members were allowed to fluctuate only within narrow bands. We consider first the case in which international capital flows respond to differences in interest rates, but not by so much as to eliminate the interest rate differential between countries. The case of perfect capital mobility, in which the volume of capital flows is so responsive to interest rate differences that they cannot occur, is reconsidered in section 5.5.

The equations of section 5.2 are maintained with the exception that equation (4) is replaced by:

$$F = LF + LB + \lambda L(R - R^*) \qquad (4a)$$

which states that the change in reserves of foreign currency is the sum of two components, namely the current account and the capital account of the balance of payments. The latter is captured as the last term on the right of equation (4a), which represents the net flow of capital last period, assumed to be proportional to the difference between domestic and foreign interest rates last period. So the model of section 5.2 with internationally immobile capital is a special case of this model, in which $\lambda = 0$.

The earlier flowgraph is modified by introducing an additional exogenous variable node for R^*, and additional arcs from R and from R^* to F with transmittances $-\lambda L$ and λL respectively. The new flowgraph is shown in Figure 5.6. The modifications have introduced an extra loop with negative loop transmittance into the system. The salient features of the model can be read straight off the flowgraph. Thus we see that changes in the domestic component of the money supply S continue to have only a short-run effect on the interest rate R and on output Y because no path goes through the accumulating node F. In the long run money is neutral: it has no real effects. However, a change in autonomous spending A, which includes fiscal policy, now has both a short- and a long-run effect on output. The new long-run effect arises because the path from A to Y now has a multiplying cofactor which includes the new non-touching loops, and which does not go to zero as L goes to one in the long-run.

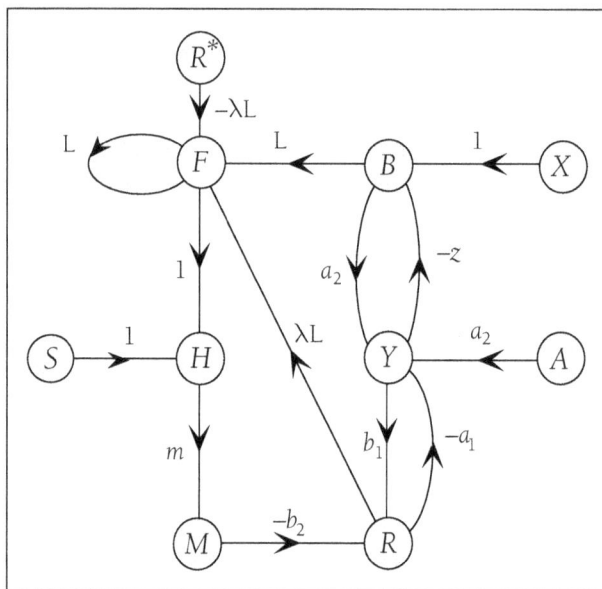

Figure 5.7 Open to trade and to capital flows

Proceeding formally to derive the consequences of changes in the exogenous variables by using Mason's rule, the system determinant is:

$$\Delta(L)=1-L+a_1b_1+a_2z+mb_2a_1zL+mb_2\lambda L+mb_2\lambda La_2z-La_1b_1-La_2z$$
$$=(1-L)(1+a_1b_1+a_2z)+mb_2L(a_1z+\lambda(1+a_2z))>0$$

Although this expression is lengthy it can be written down on inspection of the flowgraph, having noted the non-touching pairs of loops. Now we obtain any transmittances of interest by summing the cofactor-weighted direct paths and dividing by the system determinant, as shown in Table 5.3.

To:	Y	R
From:		
A	$\dfrac{a_2(1-L+mb_2\lambda L)}{\Delta(L)}$	$\dfrac{a_2b_1(1-L)+a_2zmb_2L}{\Delta(L)}$
X	$\dfrac{a_2(1-L+mb_2\lambda L)+mb_2a_1L}{\Delta(L)}$	$\dfrac{a_2b_1(1-L)-mb_2L}{\Delta(L)}$
$R*$	$\dfrac{-mb_2a_1\lambda L}{\Delta(L)}$	$\dfrac{\lambda mb_2L(1+a_2z)}{\Delta(L)}$
S	$\dfrac{mb_2a_1(1-L)}{\Delta(L)}$	$\dfrac{-mb_2(1-L+a_2z-a_2zL)}{\Delta(L)}$
where $\Delta(L)=(1-L)(1+a_1b_1+a_2z)+mb_2L(a_1z+\lambda(1+a_2z))$		

Table 5.3 Transmittance formulae

Consider the short-run, or impact effects, with L = 0, and the long-run with L = 1 as two special cases of the model. Substituting these values into the expression for the system determinant we find that for the short-run model it becomes $\Delta(0)=1+a_1b_1+a_2z$, and for the long-run model it becomes $\Delta(1)=mb_2(a_1z+\lambda(1+a_2z))$. Now we can infer the short- and long-run consequences of changes in the exogenous variables by substituting in the appropriate value of L. They are given in Tables 5.4 and 5.5.

To:	Y	R
From:		
A	$a_2/\Delta(0)$	$a_2b_1/\Delta(0)$
X	$a_2/\Delta(0)$	$a_2b_1/\Delta(0)$
$R*$	0	0
S	$mb_2a_1/\Delta(0)$	$-mb_2(1+a_2z)/\Delta(0)$
where $\Delta(0)=1+a_1b_1+a_2z$		

Table 5.4 Short-run transmittances

To:	Y	R
From:		
A	$\dfrac{a_2\lambda}{a_1 z+\lambda(1+a_2 z)}$	$\dfrac{a_2 z}{a_1 z+\lambda(1+a_2 z)}$
X	$\dfrac{a_2\lambda+a_1}{a_1 z+\lambda(1+a_2 z)}$	$\dfrac{-1}{a_1 z+\lambda(1+a_2 z)}$
R*	$\dfrac{-\lambda a_1}{a_1 z+\lambda(1+a_2 z)}$	$\dfrac{\lambda(1+a_2 z)}{a_1 z+\lambda(1+a_2 z)}$
S	0	0

Table 5.5 Long-run transmittances

Often it is not the exact formula that is of interest, but the qualitative implications such as the signs and relative sizes of the transmittances. The qualitative implications of Tables 5.4 and 5.5 are unambiguous. But if we were to calculate the long-run transmittance from autonomous domestic spending to the stock of reserves of foreign currency (see Exercise 12 below) we would find an ambiguity, but one that is easy to explain with reference to the flowgraph: there are two offsetting paths. On the one hand the induced rise in imports is a drain on the reserves, but on the other hand the induced rise in the interest rate draws in capital from abroad.

Let us relate the flowgraph to the usual diagrammatic representation of this model in Y–R space, which consists of an IS-LM diagram with an added BoP line representing equilibrium in the balance of payments. The IS curve represents the single $R \rightarrow Y$ arc. It is shifted by the inflows to Y stemming from A and X. The LM curve represents the $Y \rightarrow R$ arc, which is shifted by the inflows to R via M. These inflows can arise from the dynamic process centered on F, representing accumulating reserves of foreign currency at the central bank. Thus the LM curve is not static. However, in the long-run steady state, the net inflow to F is zero, which means that the balance of trade B and net capital flows, $\lambda(R-R^*)$, are exactly offsetting. Combinations of Y and R that achieve this imply that $-X+zY=\lambda(R-R^*)$, which defines the BoP line in Y–R space. The value of λ determines the slope of the BoP line, ranging from vertical at $Y=X/z$

when $\lambda = 0$ to horizontal at $R=R^*$ as $\lambda \to \infty$ The process of dynamic adjustment until capital flows exactly offset the trade balance implies that in the long run the economy must be on the BoP line, and this is achieved by movements in the LM curve.

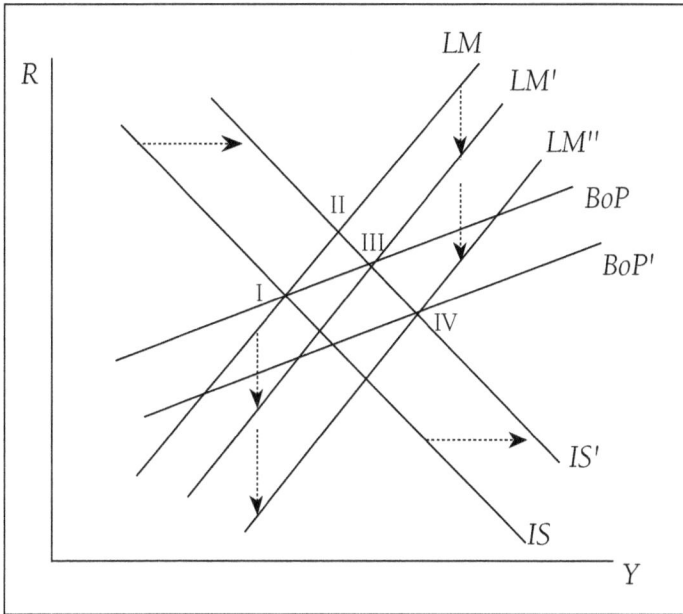

Figure 5.8 An increase in export demand

The economy is at a short term equilibrium wherever the IS and LM curves intersect in Figure 5.8, while there is a surplus in the balance of payments at all points above the BoP curve, and a deficit below it. Figure 5.8 illustrates two cases of a shift in the IS curve: (i) due to a rise in autonomous domestic spending (no change in the BoP line), and (ii) due to a rise in export demand, which involves a simultaneous shift of the BoP curve to the right. Assume that the IS curve moves to IS' in both cases. In the short run both output and the interest rate rise to the IS-LM intersection labelled II. But since the balance of payments is in surplus at that combination of R and Y, the money stock expands, driving the LM curve downwards. In the case of a rise in autonomous domestic spending, this process ceases when the LM'-IS' intersection coincides with the BoP curve at point III. However in the case of a rise in export demand, the BoP curve has also shifted to BoP' and the process continues until point IV is reached. The algebra tells us that in this case the interest rate must be lower than it was originally, and this must be for reasons similar to those discussed in the previous section on immobile capital: to maintain equilibrium in the balance of payments income must rise to stimulate sufficient imports to exactly offset the rise in exports, and this is brought about by an expansion of interest-sensitive components of aggregate expenditure, which implies a fall in the interest rate.

Setting $\lambda = 0$ yields the earlier model in which capital is immobile between countries, and setting $\lambda = \infty$ yields a model with perfectly mobile capital, to be discussed below. To derive the implications of $\lambda = \infty$ for the transmittance formulae, divide both numerator and denominator by λ. Thus compare the long-run effects on output of an increase in exports with those of an increase in autonomous domestic spending: the lower the mobility of capital flows (*i.e.* the lower is λ), the greater the difference between the long-run multipliers. If capital is perfectly mobile there is no difference at all.

Exercise 12
Derive the transmittances from the exogenous variables to *F*.

5.5   Perfectly mobile capital again

Most of the advanced market economies have dispensed with capital controls, and technological improvements together with financial liberalization mean that there are nowadays only minor impediments to the flow of portfolio capital across borders. Hence an assumption of perfectly mobile capital is the usual benchmark for open economy IS-LM models, which are generally labelled as Mundell-Fleming models. The case of perfectly mobile capital can be considered as a special case of the foregoing model as λ goes to infinity. Adopting this approach, we begin with the transmittances of Table 5.3. We shall then derive the same results by going back to the equations of the model.

Dividing both numerator and denominator in the transmittance formulae of Table 5.3 by λ, and taking the limit as $\lambda \to \infty$ yields Table 5.6.

To: From:	Y	R
A	$\dfrac{a_2}{1+a_2 z}$	0
X	$\dfrac{a_2}{1+a_2 z}$	0
$R*$	$-\dfrac{a_1}{1+a_2 z}$	1
S	0	0

Table 5.6 Transmittances when capital is perfectly mobile

We see that neither fiscal nor monetary policy affect the interest rate, which is anchored to the world interest rate R^*. Also, shocks to exports have the same impact on GDP as shocks to autonomous domestic spending. Changes in domestic monetary conditions, represented by changes in commercial banks' holdings of government securities, S, have no effect on the real variables Y and R; in fact they are exactly offset by induced changes in the central bank's reserves of foreign currency.

Note the remarkable fact that all terms involving lags have disappeared in the transmittances of Table 5.6. Thus there are no delays or dynamic effects when exogenous variables change, and the long run is the same as the short run. What has happened is that the instantaneous arbitrage of capital flows in response to interest rate differentials keeps R and R^* locked together, inverting the causal structure of the model. Thus equation (4a) has in effect been replaced by:

$$R = R^* \tag{4b}$$

and the LM equation has been rewritten as:

$$M = b_2^{-1}(R_0 - R + b_1 Y) \tag{2a}$$

meaning that the money stock is determined by the demand for money because the money supply is infinitely elasticity at the exogenous foreign interest rate. The remaining equations in the model are those for the IS equilibrium and the balance of trade:

$$Y = -a_1 R + a_2(A + B) \tag{1}$$

$$B = -zY + X \tag{3}$$

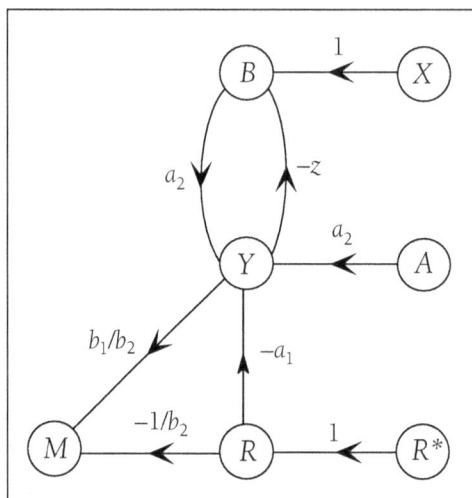

Figure 5.9 Perfectly mobile capital

The equations then produce a causal topography for a static model as shown in Figure 5.9. Note that this is the same structure—in effect the same model—as the closed economy IS-LM model with an exogenous interest rate: compare it with Figure 4.5. Coupling this Mundell-Fleming model for a small economy with a standard IS-LM model of a large economy produces the two-economy IS-LM structure discussed in Section 5.3.

Exercise 13

How should Figure 5.8 be modified to represent perfect capital mobility? From your modified diagram derive the qualitative implications given in Table 5.6

6

Flexible Exchange Rate and Mobile Capital

Although the exchange rate is flexible we maintain the assumption that the price level is fixed, which implies that the exchange rate is the real exchange rate and the interest rate continues to be the real interest rate. We are in effect considering a Mundell-Fleming model of a (small) open economy. It is customary in this context to consider the extreme case of perfect capital mobility, in which the domestic interest rate is locked equal to the world interest rate by the action of portfolio investment arbitrage. This yields a model with a simple IS-LM diagrammatic apparatus, but one in which causal processes are somewhat obscure, and for which explanation can be rather opaque as a result. Thus it is normal to find statements like this: "an expansion of the money supply tends to drive down the domestic interest rate which induces incipient outflows of capital, which depreciate the exchange rate" and so on. But we know that with perfect capital mobility the interest rate cannot move, so why would there be such "incipient outflows of capital"? Here, instead, the model is first developed with an explicit underlying dynamic process, in which there are actual flows of capital in response to an actual, as opposed to incipient, interest rate differential.

In section 6.1 it is assumed that, despite a varying exchange rate, people expect a constant "normal" level of the exchange rate, to which it is expected to revert after some deviation. This assumption allows us to bypass explicit modelling of exchange rate expectations, which would otherwise be necessary in a model in which capital flows respond to differences in the returns to assets held in different countries and in different currency denominations. A more sophisticated assumption about exchange rate expectations – namely "perfect foresight" – is intro duced in Section 6.2 which also assumes perfect capital mobility.

6.1   Static exchange rate expectations

An inflow of capital from abroad means that foreigners acquire domestic assets which are claims on future domestic income. To make such purchases they must exchange foreign currency for domestic currency. The variable F now denotes total domestic holdings of the foreign currency.

$$F = LF + LB + \lambda L(R - R^*)$$

This says that the one-period change in holdings of foreign currency at the *beginning* of a period, i.e. the balance of payments $\Delta F = (1–L)F$, equals the sum of last period's current account B and last period's capital account, which is proportional to the interest rate differential in the last period. As F increases, so the exchange value of the domestic currency increases—i.e. it appreciates. We adopt the convention that E represents the foreign currency price of a unit of domestic currency. Thus a rise in E signifies an appreciation of the domestic currency and a fall in E signifies a depreciation of the domestic currency. Thus the exchange rate E varies directly with F which we represent as a simple linear function as follows:

$$E = eF$$

and the equation for the balance of trade, or net exports, is modified to become:

$$B = B(Y,E) = B_0 - z_1 Y - z_2 E$$

showing that net exports fall as E rises. These three equations, combined with equations for the IS and LM equations, $Y = a_2(A+B) - a_1 R$ and $R = b_1 Y - b_2 M$, comprise the model for which a flowgraph representation is given in Figure 6.1.

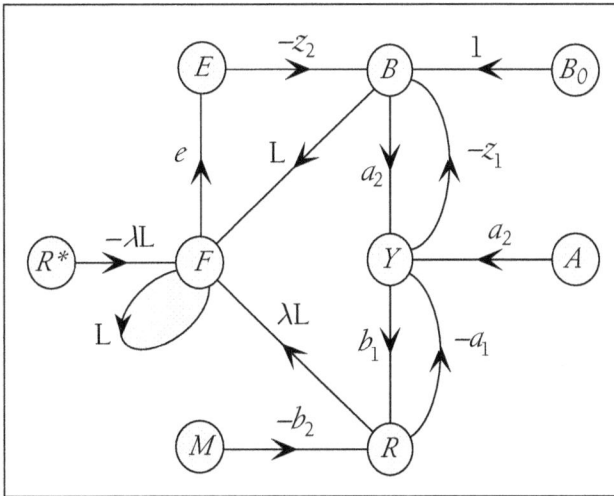

Figure 6.1: Flexible exchange rate and capital flows

The five nodes with inflowing arcs represent the five equations, and the other four nodes are exogenous variables. The essential difference between the flexible exchange rate model here and the earlier fixed exchange rate model can be seen by comparing Figure 6.1 with Figure 5.7. A capital inflow induced by a lower interest rate abroad leads in both cases to an increased supply of foreign currency F to the foreign exchange market, which in the fixed exchange rate case was purchased by the central bank in order to prevent an appreciation of the domestic currency, and consequently increased the monetary base. In the present flexible exchange rate case, the increased supply of foreign currency lowers its price, implying an appreciation of the domestic currency, i.e. E rises. Thus whereas capital flows affect the money supply and consequently shift the LM curve under fixed exchange rates, under flexible exchange rates capital flows affect the net export function B and consequently shift the IS curve. An appreciating currency lowers net exports, which lowers aggregate demand Y, so the IS curve moves leftwards.

The dynamic model and flowgraph with imperfect capital mobility has been presented in order to explain the process of adjustment. It covers a variety of cases, from zero capital mobility when $\lambda = 0$ to perfect capital mobility as $\lambda \to \infty$, but this generality makes it a little more complicated than the simple extreme of perfect capital mobility usually presented in textbooks, which is considered in the next section. The flowgraph has five loops, and three pairs of non-touching loops, giving a system determinant:

$$\Delta = (1-L)(1+a_2z_1+a_1b_1)+ez_2L(1+a_2b_1\lambda+a_1b_1)$$

Considering this as a function of the lag operator L, and evaluating it for the particular values L=0 and L=1, we find: $\Delta(0)=1+a_2z_1+a_1b_1$ and $\Delta(1)=ez_2(1+a_2b_1\lambda+a_1b_1)$. It is also useful to note that:

$$\lim_{\lambda\to\infty}\left[\frac{\Delta}{\lambda}\right]=ez_2a_2b_1L \ .$$

Table 6.1 gives general transmittance formulae derived from the flowgraph of Figure 6.1 by Mason's rule, and Tables 6.2, 6.3 and 6.4 are derived from this as special cases. They report the particular transmittances corresponding to impact effects (L=0), long run effects (L=1) and perfect capital mobility ($\lambda\to\infty$).

To	Y	R	E
From			
A	$\dfrac{a_2(1-L+ez_2L)}{\Delta}$	$\dfrac{a_2b_1(1-L+ez_2L)}{\Delta}$	$\dfrac{(b_1\lambda-z_1)a_2eL}{\Delta}$
B_0	$\dfrac{a_2(1-L)}{\Delta}$	$\dfrac{a_2b_1(1-L)}{\Delta}$	$\dfrac{(1+a_1b_1+a_2b_1\lambda)eL}{\Delta}$
R^*	$\dfrac{a_2z_2e\lambda L}{\Delta}$	$\dfrac{b_1a_2z_2e\lambda L}{\Delta}$	$\dfrac{-(1+a_1b_1+a_2z_1)e\lambda L}{\Delta}$
where $\Delta=(1-L)(1+a_2z_1+a_1b_1)+ez_2L(1+a_2b_1\lambda+a_1b_1)$			

Table 6.1 Transmittances for flexible exchange rate model

Note that the flowgraph shows that the money supply is exogenous in this model. As we shall see, monetary policy can be a potent tool of control. See exercise 14(i) below for the effects of changes in M.

The transmittances of Table 6.1 appear moderately complicated, but can easily be simplified for the short- and long-run effects they imply. To get the short-run, or impact effects of a change in an exogenous variable we set the lag operator to zero in each of these transmittances.

To	Y	R	E
From			
A	$\dfrac{a_2}{1+a_2 z_1 + a_1 b_1}$	$\dfrac{a_2 b_1}{1+a_2 z_1 + a_1 b_1}$	0
B_0	$\dfrac{a_2}{1+a_2 z_1 + a_1 b_1}$	$\dfrac{a_2 b_1}{1+a_2 z_1 + a_1 b_1}$	0
R^*	0	0	0
M	$\dfrac{b_2 a_1}{1+a_2 z_1 + a_1 b_1}$	$\dfrac{-b_2(1+a_2 z_1)}{1+a_2 z_1 + a_1 b_1}$	0

Table 6.2 Short-run (impact) effects

The zeros in Table 6.2 derive mainly from the lags in the system and the convention adopted for the timing of the measurement of stocks as being at the beginning of a period. Because, therefore, all influences on the stock of domestic holdings of foreign currency are delayed effects, any effect that works through the stock must be zero in the same-period, which is the short-run. Therefore all the non-zero entries in Table 6.2 involve paths that do not involve the stock variable (domestic holdings of foreign currency).

To	Y	R	E
From			
A	$\dfrac{a_2}{1+a_2 b_1 \lambda + a_1 b_1}$	$\dfrac{a_2 b_1}{1+a_2 b_1 \lambda + a_1 b_1}$	$\dfrac{a_2(b_1\lambda - z_1)}{z_2(1+a_2 b_1 \lambda + a_1 b_1)}$
B_0	0	0	$\dfrac{1}{z_2}$
R^*	$\dfrac{a_2 \lambda}{1+a_2 b_1 \lambda + a_1 b_1}$	$\dfrac{a_2 b_1 \lambda}{1+a_2 b_1 \lambda + a_1 b_1}$	$-\dfrac{\lambda(1+a_2 z_1 + a_1 b_1)}{z_2(1+a_2 b_1 \lambda + a_1 b_1)}$
M	$\dfrac{b_2(a_1 + a_2 \lambda)}{1+a_2 b_1 \lambda + a_1 b_1}$	$\dfrac{-b_2}{1+a_2 b_1 \lambda + a_1 b_1}$	$-\dfrac{b_2\lambda(1+a_2 z_1)+b_2 a_1 z_1}{z_2(1+a_2 b_1 \lambda + a_1 b_1)}$

Table 6.3 Long-run (equilibrium) effects

The main thing to note about Table 6.3 is the qualitative pattern of the transmittances. It is noteworthy, and perhaps somewhat surprising, that a change in the autonomous component of the balance of trade has no long-run effect on either GDP or the interest rate, whereas increased autonomous domestic demand increases both of these variables. The only ambiguous sign in Table 6.3 is the effect of autonomous domestic demand on the exchange rate. Referring to the flowgraph we can see that this is because of the two offsetting causal paths: a negative effect via the current account, and a positive effect via the capital account of the balance of payments.

To	Y	R	E
From			
A	0	0	$\dfrac{1}{z_2}$
B_0	0	0	$\dfrac{1}{z_2}$
R^*	$\dfrac{1}{b_1}$	1	$-\dfrac{1+a_1 b_1 + a_2 z_1}{z_2 a_2 b_1}$
M	$\dfrac{b_2}{b_1}$	0	$-\dfrac{b_2(1+a_2 z_1)}{z_2 a_2 b_1}$

Table 6.4 Perfectly mobile capital ($\lambda \to \infty$)

The case of perfect capital mobility shown in Table 6.4 is obtained by allowing λ in Table 6.1 to become infinitely large. To do this, first divide both the numerator and the denominator of each transmittance in Table 6.1 by λ and note that $\lambda \to \infty$ implies $1/\lambda \to 0$. When this is done all terms involving the lag operator disappear, so dynamic effects are absent in this version of the model: it has in effect been converted into a static model. Notice too that the transmittances generally differ from those of the long-run version of the imperfect capital mobility formulation.

It is left to the reader to infer the transmittances for the case of complete immobility of capital between countries, but observe that there will still be dynamic effects in this case because the trade balance continues to independently affect the supply and demand for foreign currency. It may seem rather odd to have a flexible exchange rate without capital flows between countries, but there are some circumstances in which it applies. For example, the Russian ruble in the early 1990s was floating against the major currencies, but the absence of a Russian bond market ruled out the possibility of capital flows in or out of Russia in response to interest rate differentials.

A diagrammatic analysis of the model is presented in Figure 6.2. This is an elaboration of the IS-LM diagram to include dynamics working through the balance of payments, F. In equilibrium the balance of payments is zero, meaning that there is no accumulation or decumulation of the stock of domestically held foreign currency. The BP line traces out the locus of points in Y–R space which correspond to a zero balance of payments. It must be upward-sloping because a rise in R, which induces inward flows of capital, would have to be offset by a deficit in the current account, which requires an increase in Y. Long-run equilibrium must be on this rising BP locus. But short-run equilibrium is wherever the IS and LM curves cross. The short-run is brought into line with the long-run by shifts in the IS curve which are induced by changes in the exchange rate. If the IS and LM curves cross above or to the left of the BP locus then the balance of payments is in surplus and domestic holdings of foreign currency are rising. As the increased holdings of foreign currency are converted into domestic currency in the foreign exchange market, the domestic currency appreciates. This depresses net exports, i.e. the balance of trade B, pushing the IS curve leftwards.

The situation portrayed in Figure 6.2, has an initial equilibrium at point a with the domestic interest rate above the foreign interest rate R^*. Because the interest rate differential induces capital inflows, there must be an offsetting current account deficit at a. Nevertheless this is a long-run equilibrium in the sense in which we have used the term because the overall balance of payments is zero at a. Of course, capital flows cannot persist for ever, so in a different sense of the term "long-run", in which the current account of the balance of payments is zero, a more durable equilibrium would be where $R = R^*$ and $Y=Y_1$, to the south-west of a on the BP line. Figure 6.2 shows what happens when there is an increase in an autonomous component of domestic demand. The IS curve shifts rightwards to IS' so that a new short-run equilibrium is established at b with a rise in both the interest rate and output. However there is a surplus in the balance of payments at b because it is above the BP line. Thus the exchange rate appreciates and consequently the IS curve shifts leftwards. This dynamic process continues until equilibrium is re-established on the BP line. This occurs back at the original point of departure a, since neither the BP line nor the LM line have moved.

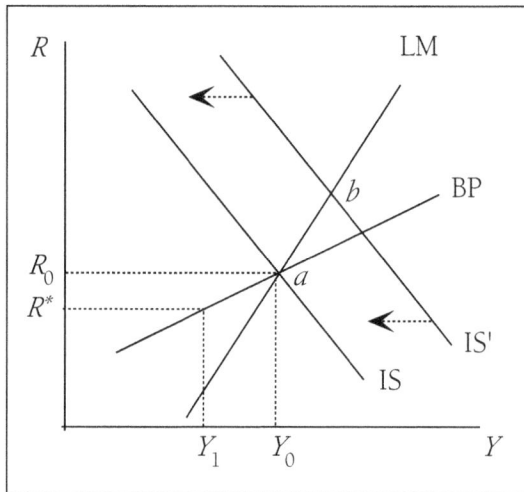

Figure 6.2: Mundell-Fleming model

Exercise 14

i. Derive the general transmittances from M to Y, R and E and confirm the M rows in Tables 6.2 to 6.4.

ii. Explain the long-run effect of an increase in export demand in this model.

iii Calculate a table of transmittances for the case of zero capital mobility.

6.2   Perfect capital mobility with perfect foresight

This is basically the same flexible exchange rate model as that of the previous section, but simplified by assuming that the response of capital flows to the expected profitability of holding assets in a particular currency is infinitely elastic. This assumption enables us to avoid explicit modelling of the capital flows and of the accumulating stocks of foreign assets which featured in the model of the previous section. The infinite elasticity of capital flows follows from an assumption that the exchange rate is expected to change in proportion to the difference in interest rates. Thus the model needs an account of exchange rate expectations. The most widely accepted way to do this is to assume that expectations about exchange rates are consistent with the predictions of the model. This is known as the assumption of "rational expectations". Here we make the stronger assumption of "perfect foresight", which is what rational expectations implies in the context of a deterministic (as opposed to stochastic) model[†].

The currency in which a holder of capital funds holds his capital will be the one in which the expected return is the greatest. Therefore the decision to hold, say, euros or US dollars depends on the difference in interest rates and on the expected change in the exchange rate. But a general expectation of a greater return in a certain currency will make it appreciate until the following condition (known as "uncovered interest parity") holds and there is no further expectation of gain:

$$\frac{E_{t+1}^e}{E_t} = \frac{1+R_t}{1+R_t^*}$$

where E_t is the this period's exchange rate, E_{t+1}^e is the expectation held this period of next period's exchange rate, R_t is this period's domestic interest rate and R_t^* is this period's foreign interest rate. All these quantities relate to the *beginning* of the relevant period. For easy analysis we pretend that all these rates move in steps over time, and only change at

---

[†]   A stochastic model with rational expectations, though not of exchange rates, is presented in Chapter 8.

the beginning of a period. Now we take logarithms of both sides of the uncovered interest parity condition to get:

$$\ln E^e_{t+1} - \ln E_t = \ln(1+R_t) - \ln(1+R_t^*)$$

or $\qquad \varepsilon^e_{t+1} - \varepsilon_t \approx R_t - R_t^*$

where $\varepsilon \equiv \ln E$ and we use the approximation $R \approx \ln(1+R)$ which is accurate for small values of R. If the exchange rate expectations are correct (perfect foresight) then ε^e_{t+1} can be replaced by ε_{t+1}:

$$\varepsilon_{t+1} - \varepsilon_t \approx R_t - R_t^*,$$

and lagging by one period we get: $\varepsilon_t - \varepsilon_{t-1} \approx R_{t-1} - R_{t-1}^*$. This is the condition we add (as an equality instead of an approximation) to a simple IS-LM-BoP model:

$$Y = -a_1 R + a_2(A+B)$$
$$B = B_0 - z_1 Y - z_2 \varepsilon$$
$$\varepsilon = L\varepsilon + LR - LR^*$$
$$R = b_1 Y - b_2 M$$

where the various symbols have the same meaning as in the previous section. The exogenous variables are: A, B_0, R^* and M. The causal flow-graph shown in Figure 6.3 is determined by this assignment of exogeneity. It can be seen that there are four loops and two pairs of non-touching loops in this flowgraph. From these we get the system determinant:

$$\Delta(L) = 1 - L + a_1 b_1 + a_2 z_1 + a_2 b_1 z_2 L - a_1 b_1 L - a_2 z_1 L$$
$$= (1-L)(1 + a_1 b_1 + a_2 z_1) + a_2 b_1 z_2 L$$

where the first term on the right hand side goes to zero in the long-run and the second term goes to zero in the short-run, i.e.

$$\Delta(0) = 1 + a_1 b_1 + a_2 z_1 \quad \text{and} \quad \Delta(1) = a_2 b_1 z_2.$$

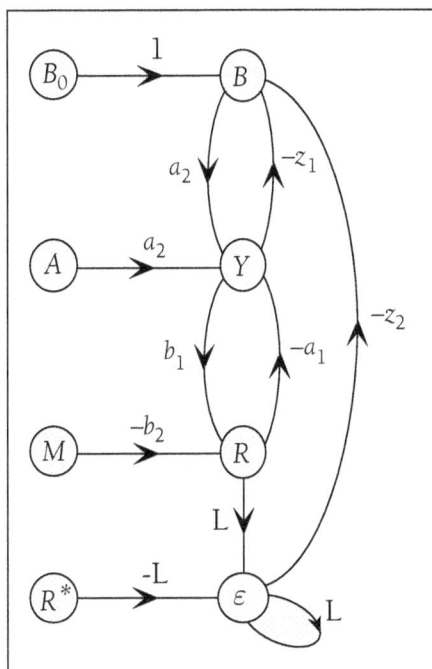

Figure 6.3: Simple Mundell-Fleming model

Hence we can derive the effects of unit increases in the exogenous variables, *i.e.* the transmittances shown in Tables 6.5 to 6.7.

To	Y	R	E
From			
A	$\dfrac{a_2(1-L)}{\Delta}$	$\dfrac{a_2 b_1(1-L)}{\Delta}$	$\dfrac{b_1 a_2 L}{\Delta}$
B_0	$\dfrac{a_2(1-L)}{\Delta}$	$\dfrac{a_2 b_1(1-L)}{\Delta}$	$\dfrac{a_2 b_1 \lambda L}{\Delta}$
R^*	$\dfrac{a_2 z_2 L}{\Delta}$	$\dfrac{b_1 a_2 z_2 L}{\Delta}$	$\dfrac{-(1+a_1 b_1+a_2 z_1)L}{\Delta}$
M	$\dfrac{b_2 a_2 z_2 L+b_2 a_1(1-L)}{\Delta}$	$\dfrac{-b_2(a_2 z_1(1-L))}{\Delta}$	$\dfrac{-b_2 L(1+a_2 z_1)}{\Delta}$

Table 6.5: General transmittances for Mundell-Fleming model

To	Y	R	E
From			
A	$\dfrac{a_2}{1+a_2 z_1 + a_1 b_1}$	$\dfrac{a_2 b_1}{1+a_2 z_1 + a_1 b_1}$	0
B_0	$\dfrac{a_2}{1+a_2 z_1 + a_1 b_1}$	$\dfrac{a_2 b_1}{1+a_2 z_1 + a_1 b_1}$	0
R^*	0	0	0
M	$\dfrac{b_2 a_1}{1+a_2 z_1 + a_1 b_1}$	$\dfrac{-b_2(1+a_2 z_1)}{1+a_2 z_1 + a_1 b_1}$	0

Table 6.6: Mundell-Fleming: short-run (impact) effects

To	Y	R	E
From			
A	0	0	$\dfrac{1}{z_2}$
B_0	0	0	$\dfrac{1}{z_2}$
R^*	$\dfrac{1}{b_1}$	1	$-\dfrac{1+a_1 b_1 + a_2 z_1}{z_2 a_2 b_1}$
M	$\dfrac{b_2}{b_1}$	0	$-\dfrac{b_2(1+a_2 z_1)}{z_2 a_2 b_1}$

Table 6.7: Mundell-Fleming: long-run effects

Let us consider the effects of fiscal and monetary policies as examples to illustrate the transmittances shown in Tables 6.6 and 6.7, in other words the top and bottom rows of the tables. The standard analysis depicts these in the Y–R space of an IS-LM diagram, as displayed in Figure 6.4. Starting in equilibrium at point a, a fiscal expansion is shown in part (i), and a monetary expansion is shown in part (ii). The immediate, short-run change is shown by a solid arrow and the (gradual) long-run effect by a dashed arrows. Thus a fiscal expansion shifts the IS curve to the right, producing a new temporary equilibrium at point *b*, with both output and the domestic interest rate increased. But now the gap between the domestic interest rate and the world interest rate implies that the exchange rate must appreciate which reduces net exports and hence total expenditure and output. Thus the IS curve moves leftwards until it eventually arrives back at *a* with no change in either Y or R. However it would not be correct to say that in the end

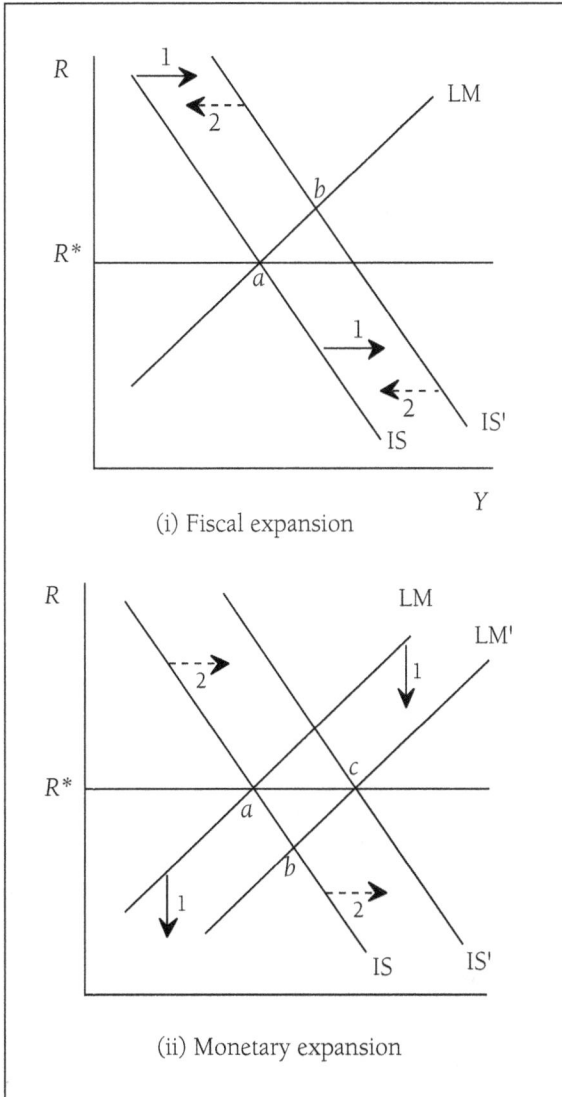

(i) Fiscal expansion

(ii) Monetary expansion

Figure 6.4 Short- and long-run effects of macroeconomic policies

nothing has changed because although GDP has returned to its initial values, the *composition* of GDP has changed: the fiscal increase in expenditure is exactly offset by a reduction in net exports. This has been brought about by the rise in the exchange rate, which is explicit in the transmittances derived from the flowgraph, but can also be inferred from the IS-LM diagram by recalling that the exchange rate was rising during the whole period when the domestic interest rate exceeded the world interest rate, $R > R^*$.

In the case of a monetary expansion, which shifts the LM curve downwards, the exchange rate depreciates so long as the new equilibrium at b lies below the R^* line. This increases net exports, which causes the IS curve to move rightwards until a new equilibrium is attained at point c. Thus GDP has increased, initially in part due to the fall in the interest rate, but eventually entirely due to the improvement in the net foreign balance.

It is instructive to compare the Mundell-Fleming model of this section with that of the previous section. Note that Table 6.7 is identical to Table 6.4. The flowgraph of Figure 6.3 can be derived from that of Figure 6.1 by (i) absorbing the F node, (ii) setting $\lambda e = 1$ and (iii) making λ infinitely large ($\lambda \to \infty$) so that e vanishes ($e \to 0$). Operation (i) does not change the earlier model at all, but operations (ii) and (iii) substantially constrain it. Setting $\lambda e = 1$ simply reflects the fact that investors who hold foreign currency are indifferent as to whether their return comes from an interest rate differential or an (expected) exchange rate appreciation: the interest rate differential which induces a flow of capital which in turn changes the exchange rate would be a one-way bet for arbitrageurs if the change in the exchange rate were not exactly equal to the original interest rate differential. The condition $\lambda e = 1$ ensures that such unlimited arbitrage gains are ruled out. Then making λ infinitely large effectively decouples net exports B from any influence on the exchange rate, because the BP line in Figure 6.2 becomes horizontal at the foreign interest rate R^*, and the exchange rate is now solely determined by capital flows.

7

The Price Level and Inflation

7.1 Aggregate demand

The IS-LM model determines equilibrium values of variables such as the level of national income and the rate of interest in real terms. Since the price level is taken as given, it is not necessary to distinguish between nominal and real measures of GNP, nor between nominal and real interest rates. However, although the aggregate price level and its rate of change, the rate of inflation, are determined outside the IS-LM model, they do affect the variables that are determined within it. The channels of influence from the price level to the determination of real variables are encapsulated within the heading "aggregate demand". The aggregate demand schedule describes how real national income responds to a change in the price level. It is one of the reduced form relationships implicit in the IS-LM model.

Two of the mechanisms by which the price level affects real variables were first set out by Pigou and Keynes in early controversies provoked by the publication of Keynes' *General Theory*. If prices are flexible, Pigou argued, price falls make consumers better off even if wages fall in step with prices. This occurs because some part of consumers' wealth is held in assets denominated in nominal terms, like money and most government bonds. Symmetrically, a rise in the general price level makes consumers worse off. The Pigou effect therefore works directly on expenditure through a consumption function which has real wealth as an argument. Its channel of influence is in the IS part of the IS-LM model.

The Keynes effect, by contrast, works through the LM part of the model. The demand for money is properly specified in terms of real money balances, which is to say that the demand for nominal balances should be proportional to the aggregate price level. This means that a given percentage increase in the price level has the same effect as an equal percentage reduction in the supply of money: both reduce the stock of real money balances held by the public. Keynes did not believe that either mechanism, the Pigou effect or the Keynes effect, is strong, at least not in the short term. However it is nowadays recognised that a properly specified consumption function will indeed allow for intertemporal allocation of consumption by consumers, and consequently that wealth is an important determinant of consumer spending, as the Pigou effect requires. Furthermore, it is doubtful whether Keynes' views, that the interest elasticity of aggregate expenditure is very low and the interest elasticity of the demand for money is very high, can be seriously maintained nowadays in the light of numerous studies that have found significant and finite interest elasticities even in the short run.

The third channel by which the aggregate price level can influence real aggregate variables in the IS-LM model is through the trade balance, or net exports. An increase in the general price level has a direct negative influence on a country's external competitiveness, and this is reflected in both expenditure—exports fall and imports rise—and in the current account of the balance of payments. The direct effect of a fall in expenditure and income may be either reinforced or offset by indirect, dynamic effects working through the balance of payments, depending on the exchange rate regime. If the exchange rate is fixed the indirect effects reinforce the direct effect on real income, but if the exchange rate is flexible and determined in the market for foreign exchange then the indirect effects are offsetting. If the exchange rate is fixed and the balance of payments initially in equilibrium, then the indirect effects of an increase in the price level take place via a loss of reserves which reduces the stock of money, increases the interest rate and thereby induces a further fall in expenditure. This indirect channel of influence obviously relies on the same interest elasticities as the Keynes effect. On the other hand, if the exchange rate is flexible, the impact of the increased demand for foreign currency occasioned by the adverse movement in the current account depresses the exchange rate (*i.e.* the price of foreign exchange will rise), thereby tending to restore competitiveness, thus offsetting the initial direct consequences of the price rise on real income and expenditure. The exchange rate depreciation would tend to push the price level further upwards.

The three mechanisms by which the price level affects real variables are incorporated in the IS-LM model in Figure 7.1.

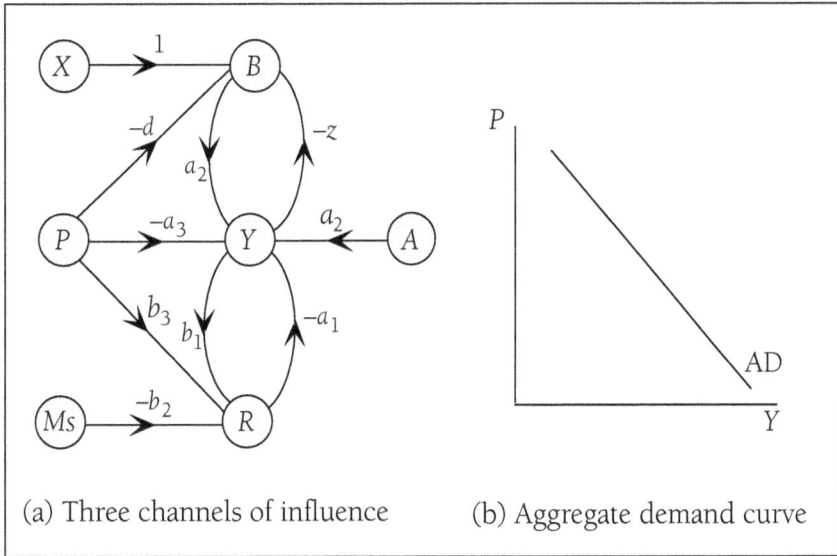

(a) Three channels of influence   (b) Aggregate demand curve

Figure 7.1 Price level and aggregate demand

Three arcs emanate from the P node, and the flowgraph assumes that P has an approximately linear effect on B, Y and R. Be that as it may, it is the sign of the overall effect on Y that is of most interest, and the combined effect of three negative paths allows us to draw the aggregate demand curve with a negative slope.

The aggregate demand curve summarises all the channels through which the price level affects output Y. Note that it subsumes the whole IS-LM model. Variations in the other exogenous variables, X, M^s and A also impinge on Y as the flowgraph shows, and the signs of their transmittances to Y tell how they shift the AD curve. Thus increases in exports or in autonomous domestic spending or in the money supply all shift the AD curve rightwards.

The slope of the aggregate demand curve is the inverse of the transmittance from P to Y, namely $-(1+b_1a_1+a_2z)/(da_2+a_3+b_3a_1)$. It is a complicated function of the parameters in the model, and many of the parameters in this expression are themselves functions of other more basic parameters like the marginal propensity to consume c and the marginal tax rate t. But it can be seen that it would need an exceptional set of values for these parameters to produce a vertical AD curve, essentially requiring the denominator in the slope expression to be zero. From what was said earlier about the differences between a fixed exchange rate regime and a flexible exchange rate regime for the balance of payments effect, we can infer that the long-run AD curve is steeper in a regime of flexible exchange rates.

The flowgraph in Figure 7.1 shows that a positive shock to the price level has an ambiguous overall effect on the rate of interest. Two channels, the Pigou effect and the balance of payments effect, tend to push the rate of interest downwards, while the Keynes effect working through the demand for money tends to push it upwards.

7.2   Sticky price dynamics

In this and in subsequent sections we shall be working with logarithmically transformed variables. The reason for this is that that the price level can be arbitrarily scaled, so that it can be measured by an index, and it is the *proportional change* in the price level (*i.e.* inflation) that matters. Proportional changes translate into simple differences when the variable is measured in logarithms. Another advantage of working in logarithms is that the parameters of functions that are linear in logarithms are elasticities, which helps interpretation. Furthermore, when a variable is growing at a constant rate over time it is growing exponentially, but the logarithm of that variable is growing linearly. All this aids tractability. Against this must be set the fact that some key relationships, such as the $Y = C+I+G$ identity, are linear in the levels of the variables.

However, taking the model as a whole, and on the basis that it represents only an approximation to the system under examination, it seems acceptable to give a log-linear approximation as the reduced form of the IS submodel if our main focus is elsewhere in the system. Hence the IS equilibrium is written:

$$y = -a_1 R + a_2 x \qquad (1)$$

where y is the logarithm of income, R is the real interest rate as before and x is the logarithm of autonomous components of expenditure. This implies that output has an interest semi-elasticity of $-a_1$ and an expenditure elasticity of a_2.

We now develop the IS-LM-AD model by modifying the assumption that the price level is exogenous. Instead, the price level is "predetermined" in any period, but adjusts gradually between periods according to the difference between the level of aggregate demand and the natural level of output. A model of this kind features in the textbook of Hall and Taylor.[†]

$$p_t = p_{t-1} + d(y_{t-1} - y^*_{t-1})$$

where p is the logarithm of the price level, and y^* is the natural level of output. Using the lag operator L, we re-express this as:

$$p = Lp + d(Ly - Ly^*) . \qquad (1)$$

Textbook exposition normally proceeds in terms of an aggregate demand curve in which the price level shifts the LM curve, based on the Keynes effect. Following this, the inverse money demand function is now expressed in terms of the demand for real balances:

$$R = R_0 + b_1 y - b_2(m - p) \qquad (2)$$

where m is the logarithm of the money stock. The underlying demand function for real balances has a constant interest semi-elasticity, and a constant output elasticity.

In Figure 7.2 the transmittance of the self-loop on p is simply the lag operator, L. It implies that the price level changes whenever there is any input to that node, i.e. whenever $y - y^*$ is non-zero. Hence the explana-

---

[†] R. E. Hall and J. B. Taylor, *Macroeconomics*, 1998, New York: Norton.

tion for change and equilibrium in this model centers on adjustment to aggregate demand y. With aggregate demand greater that natural output y*, the induced increase in the price level reduces real money balances which increases the interest rate which in turn reduces aggregate demand until it equates with natural output. In terms of an IS-LM diagram, the IS schedule corresponds to the path from R to y, which does not change. However, the LM schedule corresponds to the two paths from y to R, one of which passes through p, whose movements in the adjustment process cause the schedule to shift. When p is rising the LM schedule is shifting upwards.

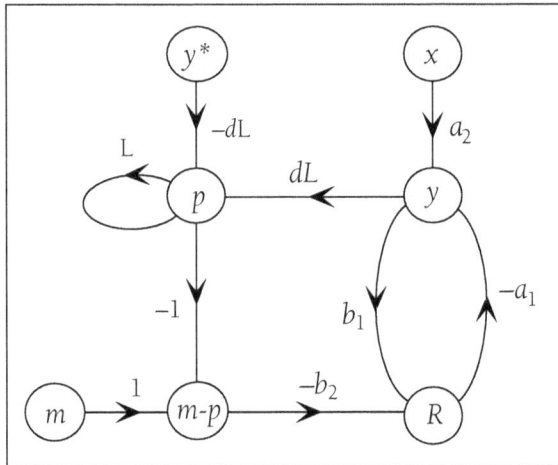

Figure 7.2: Aggregate demand with sticky prices

Alternatively the model can be pictured in Y-P space in which the path from P to Y represents the aggregate demand curve. As it contains no dynamic elements, it does not move in the process of adjustment. As P changes the economy moves along its aggregate demand curve until it reaches the intersection with aggregate supply or natural output, which does not depend on P and so is a vertical line.

The system determinant is $\Delta(L) = 1 + a_1 b_1 + a_1 d b_2 L - L - a_1 b_1 L$, where the final term is the product of the two non-touching loops. From the flowgraph we can write down the transmittances shown in Tables 7.1 and 7.2.

Exogenous variables	Endogenous variables		
	y	p	R
x	$\dfrac{a_2(1-L)}{\Delta(L)}$	$\dfrac{a_2 dL}{\Delta(L)}$	$\dfrac{a_2(b_1(1-L)+b_2 dL)}{\Delta(L)}$
y^*	$\dfrac{b_2 a_1 dL}{\Delta(L)}$	$\dfrac{-dL(1+b_1 a_1)}{\Delta(L)}$	$\dfrac{-b_2 dL}{\Delta(L)}$
m^s	$\dfrac{b_2 a_1(1-L)}{\Delta(L)}$	$\dfrac{b_2 a_1 dL}{\Delta(L)}$	$\dfrac{-b_2(1-L)}{\Delta(L)}$
where $\Delta(L)=(1-L)(1+a_1 b_1)+a_1 db_2 L$.			

Table 7.1 Transmittances in the sticky price AD model

Exogenous variables	Endogenous variables		
	y	p	R
short-run effects			
x	$\dfrac{a_2}{1+a_1 b_1}$	0	$\dfrac{a_2 b_1}{1+a_1 b_1}$
y^*	0	0	0
m^s	$\dfrac{b_2 a_1}{1+a_1 b_1}$	0	$\dfrac{-b_2}{1+a_1 b_1}$
long-run effects			
x	0	$\dfrac{a_2}{a_1 b_2}$	$\dfrac{a_2}{a_1}$
y^*	1	$\dfrac{-1-b_1 a_1}{a_1 b_2}$	$-\dfrac{1}{a_1}$
m^s	0	1	0

Table 7.2 Short- and long-run effects in the sticky price AD model

The short- and long-run effects of changes in the exogenous variables are derived from the general transmittances by setting L to zero and one respectively. These are shown in Table 7.2. A first-cut analysis of this model would look at the patterns of zeros, ones and signs shown Table 7.2, which characterise the qualitative short- and long-run behaviour of the model. For many purposes that would be sufficient, and the algebraic coefficients would be of second-order importance. Let us consider how these patterns can be read off the flowgraph. In the case of short-run effects, we note that any path that contains a multiplicative L goes to zero since the effects of that path are delayed. This gives the five zeros in the upper half of Table 7.2. Moreover, we can ignore all the loops containing a multiplicative L, and infer for example that the government spending multiplier is the same as that of the simple IS-LM model, and similarly for all the other non-zero short-run transmittances.

Now consider the pattern of qualitative long-run effects in the lower half of Table 7.2. A key factor is the self-loop on p. Consolidated into the arcs that lead into p, it multiplies them by $(1-L)^{-1}$ which goes to infinity as L goes to one, characterizing the long-run case. Similarly the loop containing one of these arcs, from y to p, also has a transmittance going to infinity. These two factors dominate any other effects, which can be ignored. This means that any path that does not include the p node has a long-run transmittance of zero, as can be seen from the three zero entries in the lower half of Table 7.2. Noting that $\Delta(1) = a_1 d b_2$, and restricting attention to paths that include the p node, we see for instance that the long-run transmittance from m to p is $a_1 b_2 d / a_1 b_2 d = 1$. A similar calculation gives the long-run transmittance from autonomous spending x to R as $a_2 b_2 d / a_1 b_2 d = a_2 / a_1$. However, care must be taken to include the cofactors of paths which do not touch certain loops. An example is the path from y^* to p, which does not touch the y-R loop, and so needs the $(1 + a_1 b_1)$ cofactor to multiply its direct transmittance.

The standard diagrammatic representation of this model is shown in Figure 7.3. Part (i) shows the effect of a shift in aggregate demand, which might reflect a change in government spending or in the money supply. Part (ii) shows the effect of a shift in the natural level of output y^* or aggregate supply. An increase in aggregate demand brings about an immediate expansion of output followed by a gradual rise in prices and decline in output along the new AD$_2$ locus. A shift in aggregate supply induces a gradual fall in prices and a concurrent rise in output.

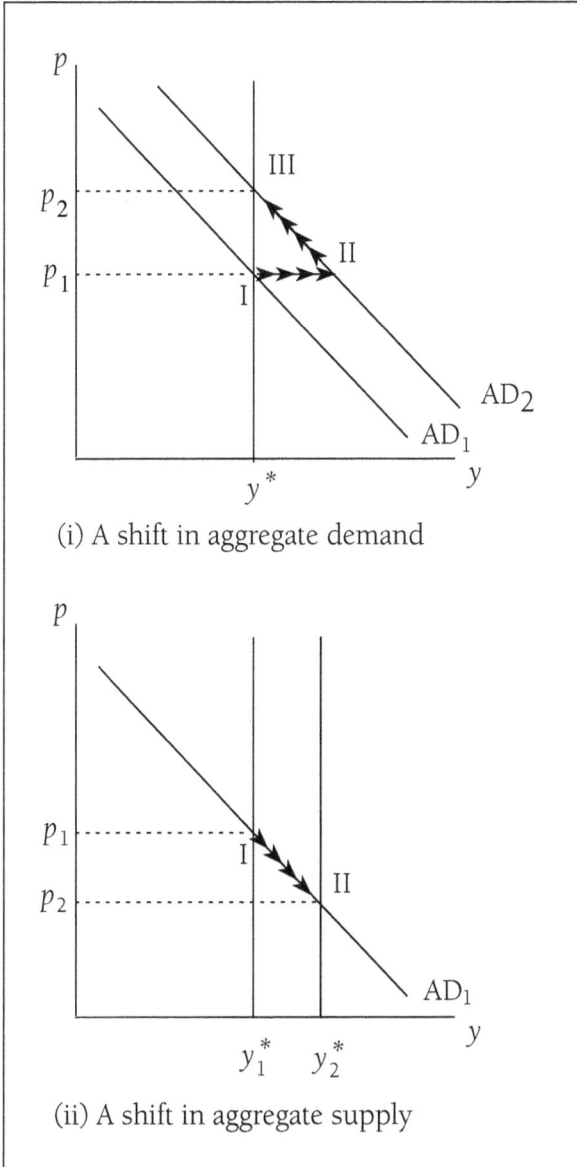

(i) A shift in aggregate demand

(ii) A shift in aggregate supply

Fig. 7.3 Aggregate demand and sticky (predetermined) price

> **Exercise 15**
>
> Adapt the model of this section to distinguish explicitly between the real and nominal interest rates, where $i = R + \pi$, and assume that output depends on the real interest rate R while the demand for money depends on the nominal interest rate i. Assume that the rate of money growth μ is exogenous, $m = Lm + \mu$. How does an increase in μ affect inflation, output and the real interest rate in the long-run?

7.3. Steady Inflation

In a steady state all variables are growing at a constant rate (which may not be the same for each variable, but will often imply that some variables grow at a common constant rate of zero, and other variables grow at a common non-zero constant rate). Thus the logarithms of variables vary over time along a straight line, with slope equal to the growth rate.

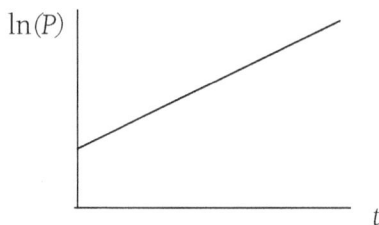

Assuming a constant population and no technical progress (so no growth in real output), steady monetary growth implies a steady rate of inflation, equal to the rate of money growth: $\Delta m_t = \pi_t \equiv \Delta \ln p_t$. We expect that all real variables—the level of real income, the real interest rate *etc.*—will not vary across steady states with different rates of inflation. Since prices grow at the same rate as money, real money balances are constant. However, they are not invariant across steady states.

In an inflationary environment, with prices rising and expected to rise, we must distinguish the real and nominal rates of interest. They are connected to the anticipated rate of inflation by the Fisher equation, $\pi^e = i - R$. Now the appropriate rate of interest for the money demand function is the opportunity cost of keeping assets as money—*i.e.* the

nominal rate i, while the appropriate rate of interest for the expenditure
function (investment and consumption) is the real rate, R. This means
that in different inflationary steady states there will be different levels of
real money balances. The output level is given by real factors—the
production function and the supply and demand for labour—so we may
write down a model for the (long-run) steady inflation economy as:

$$y = a_0 - a_1(i - \pi^e) \qquad \text{IS} \qquad (1)$$

$$m - p = b_1 y - b_2 i \qquad \text{LM} \qquad (2)$$

$$y = y^* \qquad \text{aggregate supply} \qquad (3)$$

$$\Delta m = \mu \qquad \text{constant money growth} \qquad (4)$$

$$\pi^e = \mu \qquad \text{steady state} \qquad (5)$$

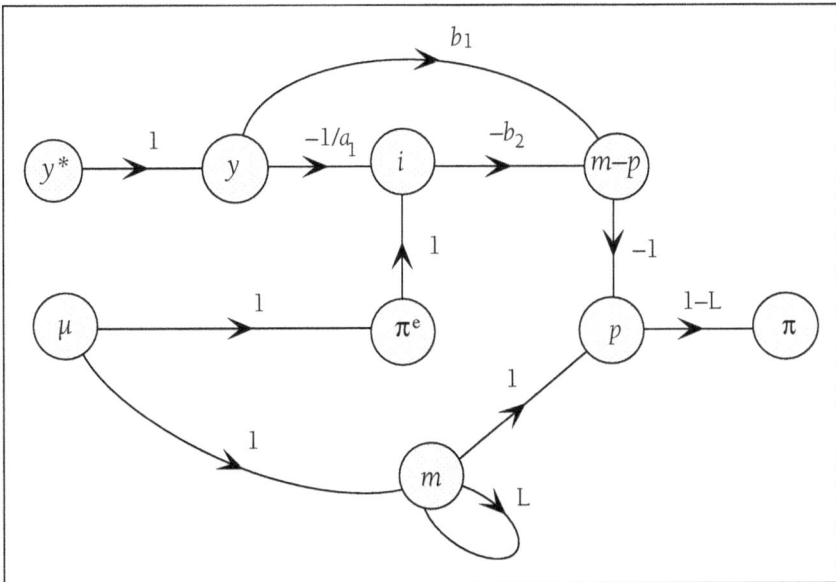

Figure 7.4: Steady state inflation

The causal structure of this long-run static model is as follows: expenditure is determined by output, and inflation is steady and equal to
the exogenous growth rate of the money stock, so the IS equation determines the nominal interest rate at the level at which aggregate de-

mand is equal to output. The LM equation determines the stock of real balances, which means it determines the price level since the stock of money is exogenous. If there is a once for all increase in the rate of money growth, then expected inflation increases by the same amount, and so does the nominal interest rate. This induces a *fall* in the stock of real balances, implying that the price level must rise faster than money until the new level of real money balances is established.

Suppose that at time t^*, after a long period of steady (hence expected) money growth and inflation, there is a surprise increase in the growth rate of the money stock, which is expected to be kept constant thereafter. After t^* the nominal interest rate must be higher, and the equilbrium stock of real balances must be lower, implying a jump in the price level.

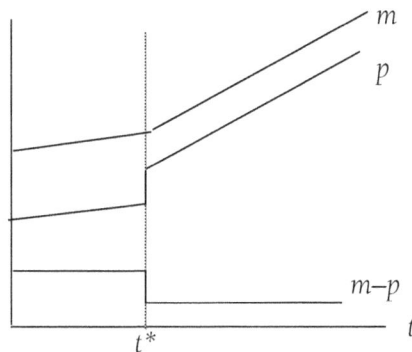

The diagram is a schematic representation of the steady states before and after the change. The slopes of the m and p curves represent their growth rates, which are equal throughout, except for the jump at time t^*. But since the model only represents steady states, the jump should not be interpreted literally—it may instead imply that for a transitional period inflation exceeds the growth rate of m, though they will eventually converge.

Exercise 16

Derive the "impact" and long-run responses of p and π to step increases in μ and y^* from the flowgraph of Figure 7.4

7.4 The Cagan model with adaptive expectations

Real variables are completely suppressed in the Cagan model, which only concerns money and prices. This makes it particularly apt for high- or hyper-inflation economies, where the effects of changes in real variables on the price level are swamped by the inflation process. In such an economy, the real interest rate is small compared with the nominal rate and variations in the real interest rate are also small compared with those of expected inflation, so it is not unreasonable to express the demand for real balances in terms of the expected rate of inflation alone:

$$m - p = \gamma - \alpha \pi^e + u.$$

where u is a shock to the money demand function.

How can inflationary expectations be modelled? This was an issue that Cagan had to confront, and in doing so he brought the concept of adaptive expectations into being. In its day this was a very significant innovation which, though it has since been superceded by the concept of rational expectations, enables tractable models to yield interesting and testable predictions. In the present context it may be expressed in the proposition that the expected rate of inflation changes in proportion to the latest prediction error:

$$\pi^e(1 - L) = \lambda((1 - L)p - L\pi^e) \quad \text{i.e.} \quad \Delta\pi_t^e = \lambda(\pi_t - \pi_{t-1}^e)$$

or $\quad \pi^e = \lambda(1 - L)p + (1 - \lambda)L\pi^e \quad$ i.e. $\quad \pi_t^e = \lambda\pi_t + (1 - \lambda)\pi_{t-1}^e$

In which the parameter λ is the speed of adjustment. If $\lambda = 0$ then inflationary expectations are constant, no matter how the price level behaves. But at the other extreme, as $\lambda \to 1$ then inflationary expectations are "extrapolative" and the current rate is expected to continue.

The model is completed with an equation determining the money supply. Here we assume a constant growth of the money supply:

$$m = \mu + Lm.$$

The causal structure of the model is shown in Figure 7.5. The stock of real money balances, $m-p$, is a key variable to understand in this model, so we consider how real money balances are affected by a change in the growth rate of the money supply.

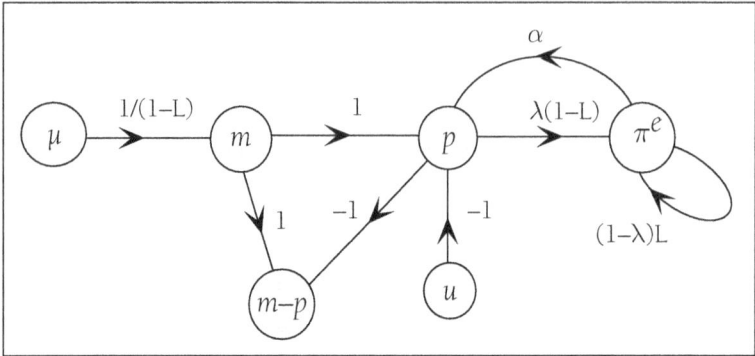

Figure 7.5: Cagan model with adaptive expectations

Note that the system determinant is: $\Delta = 1-(1-\lambda)L-\alpha\lambda(1-L)$. So the transmittance is:

$$\left\langle\frac{m-p}{\mu}\right\rangle(L) = \frac{\Delta-1+(1-\lambda)L}{(1-L)\Delta} \quad,$$

hence in the short-run: $\left\langle\dfrac{m-p}{\mu}\right\rangle(0) = \dfrac{-\alpha\lambda}{1-\alpha\lambda}$

and in the long-run: $\left\langle\dfrac{m-p}{\mu}\right\rangle(1) = -\alpha$.

thus real balances fall when the rate of money growth is increased. Since α is the (absolute value of) the interest elasticity of demand for real balances, which is generally taken to lie between 0 and -.2, and λ lies between 0 and 1, the initial drop in real balances may be smaller or larger than the eventual drop. The Cagan model is considered again in Chapter 8, with rational expectations instead of adaptive expectations.

Exercise 17

Find the effect of an increase in the rate of growth of the money supply on the rate of inflation.

7.5 The AS-AD model

Up to this point aggregate supply has been assumed to be fixed at the natural rate of output, y^*. But there is a strong supposition in modern macroeconomics that aggregate supply in fact varies in the short-run in response to variations in the difference between expected and actual prices. The idea goes back to the Friedman-Phelps reformulation of the Phillips curve to incorporate expected inflation. Indeed the expectations-augmented Phillips curve can be interpreted as an aggregate supply curve. Various theoretical explanations have been proposed for an upward-sloping aggregate supply curve in P-Y space, but we shall simply take it as granted, and given by the following equation:

$$y^S = y^* + \beta(p - p^e).$$

This is combined with the aggregate demand curve of Section 7.1:

$$y^D = A - \varphi p$$

together with an equation stating that the rate of inflation $\pi = \Delta p$ is proportional to the difference between aggregate demand and aggregate supply:

$$\Delta p = \delta(y^D - y^S).$$

In this simple model a shift in aggregate demand for whatever cause —e.g. monetary or fiscal policy—is captured by a change in A, while a shift in aggregate supply is captured by a change in y^* which is still interpreted as the "natural rate of output". The key aspect of the model is the expectations process for the price level.

The simple truth about expectations formation is that as an empirical matter there is not much to go on. The idea of adaptive expectations appears to be a successful predictor of the behaviour of some creatures under experimental conditions, but is easily shown to be inadequate for human beings who have some understanding of the processes which they are trying to predict. Here we allow for a variety of expectations formation processes captured by the following equation:

$$p^e = \lambda(L)p$$

where we consider four different forms which the function $\lambda(L)$ may take:

(i) $\lambda(L) = 0$ static expectations;
(ii) $\lambda(L) = 1$ perfect foresight;
(iii) $\lambda(L) = L$ extrapolative expectations;
(iv) $\lambda(L) = \gamma L / (1 - L + \gamma L)$ adaptive expectations.

In the next chapter we also consider rational expectations for this model.

The flowgraph for this AD-AS model can be represented as in Figure 7.6.

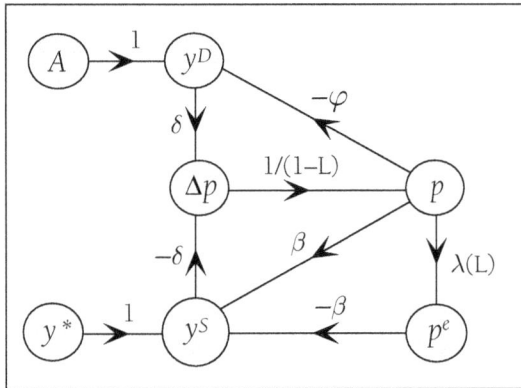

Figure 7.6: Simple AS-AD model

The effects of shifts in aggregate demand and supply on output and the price level are easily calculated from the flowgraph. They are summarised in Table 7.3.

Exogenous variables	Endogenous variables	
	p	y^s
A	$\dfrac{\delta}{1-L+(\varphi+\beta)\delta-\beta\delta\lambda(L)}$	$\dfrac{\delta\beta(1-\lambda(L))}{1-L+(\varphi+\beta)\delta-\beta\delta\lambda(L)}$
y^*	$\dfrac{-\delta}{1-L+(\varphi+\beta)\delta-\beta\delta\lambda(L)}$	$\dfrac{1-L+\varphi\delta}{1-L+(\varphi+\beta)\delta-\beta\delta\lambda(L)}$

Table 7.3 Transmittances in the simple AS-AD model

Now let us examine the four different models of expectations formation given above as cases (i) to (iv). The outcomes are summarised in Table 7.4, which is derived by substituting the appropriate formula for

$\lambda(L)$ from the relevant expectations model. Consider the short-run outcomes first. Regarding the price level, an increase in aggregate demand pushes prices up in all models whereas an increase in the natural rate of output reduces the price level in all models. Further, we see that these effects are the same in three of the models (static, extrapolative and adaptive), while the outcomes of the perfect foresight model. are different.

	Effects of a unit step increase in A			
	Short run (L = 0)		Long run (L = 1)	
Effect on:	p	y^s	p	y^s
Static	$\dfrac{\delta}{1+(\varphi+\beta)\delta}$	$\dfrac{\delta\beta}{1+(\varphi+\beta)\delta}$	$\dfrac{1}{\varphi+\beta}$	$\dfrac{\beta}{\varphi+\beta}$
Perfect foresight	$\dfrac{\delta}{1+\varphi\delta}$	0	$\dfrac{1}{\varphi}$	0
Extrapolative	$\dfrac{\delta}{1+(\varphi+\beta)\delta}$	$\dfrac{\delta\beta}{1+(\varphi+\beta)\delta}$	$\dfrac{1}{\varphi}$	0
Adaptive	$\dfrac{\delta}{1+(\varphi+\beta)\delta}$	$\dfrac{\delta\beta}{1+(\varphi+\beta)\delta}$	$\dfrac{1}{\varphi}$	0
	Effects of a unit step increase in y^*			
	Short run (L = 0)		Long run (L = 1)	
Effect on:	p	y^s	p	y^s
Static	$\dfrac{-\delta}{1+(\varphi+\beta)\delta}$	$\dfrac{1+\varphi\delta}{1+(\varphi+\beta)\delta}$	$\dfrac{-1}{\varphi+\beta}$	$\dfrac{\varphi}{\varphi+\beta}$
Perfect foresight	$\dfrac{-\delta}{1+\varphi\delta}$	1	$-\dfrac{1}{\varphi}$	1
Extrapolative	$\dfrac{-\delta}{1+(\varphi+\beta)\delta}$	$\dfrac{1+\varphi\delta}{1+(\varphi+\beta)\delta}$	$-\dfrac{1}{\varphi}$	1
Adaptive	$\dfrac{-\delta}{1+(\varphi+\beta)\delta}$	$\dfrac{1+\varphi\delta}{1+(\varphi+\beta)\delta}$	$-\dfrac{1}{\varphi}$	1

Table 7.4 Effects of different models of expectations

The perfect foresight model produces absolutely larger short-term price effects than the other three models. Regarding output, again the static, extrapolative and adaptive models yield the same positive short-term responses to an increase in aggregate demand, and also to an increase in the natural rate of output. But the short-term output response of the perfect foresight model is starkly different, both from the other models, and also in terms of the source of the exogenous change. It implies that an increase in aggregate demand has no effect on output in the short-run, whereas there is a one-for-one increase with an increase the natural rate.

Now consider the long-run outcomes. The qualitative sign pattern of effects shown in Table 7.4 is the same across all models of expectations formation. But there is a different pattern of agreement of the algebraic effects: three models produce identical outcomes, but the odd model is now that of static expectations. It results in weaker effects on the price level than the other three models. Also, its output response is weaker regarding an increase in the natural rate of output. Furthermore it shows a positive response to an increase in aggregate demand whereas no effect is recorded for the other models.

Exercise 18

Derive the effects of changes in A and y^* on y^D in the short- and long run for the four models of expectations formation considered above.

8

Simple Rational Expectations Models

8.1 Rational expectations[†]

The problem with many hypotheses about expectations is that when they are incorporated in a model they imply that the agents in the model make systematic errors, implying that agents form expectations about some variables which are not the same as the values produced ("predicted") by the model. This means that agents cannot be aware of the model. Since errors are costly, it would be in their interests to find out about the model, if it is correct.

For example, in a model which assumes that agents form adaptive expectations about inflation, if the growth of the money supply is constantly increasing, then expected inflation is always less than actual inflation. Surely rational agents would cotton on! If so, the adaptive expectations formulation is not appropriate. Actions based on adaptive expectations are costly to the individuals who make them. Purposeful agents—i.e. utility maximizing individuals and profit maximizing firms —will avoid making such errors.

We can easily write down a deterministic model in which agents do not make expectational errors by equating the expectation of a variable with its actual value. Such a model is a "perfect foresight" model. By definition, there are no expectational errors in such a model. A less stringent model is one in which expectational errors are made, but in

---

[†] This chapter draws on the presentation of rational expectations models set out in
B. T. MacCallum, *Monetary Economics*, 1989, Macmillan: New York.

which there is nothing systematic about the errors, so that the predictions cannot be improved upon. Such a "rational expectations" model must be stochastic.

The concept of expectations used here is the "mathematical expectation", or mean, of the distribution of a random variable. Thus consider the discrete uniform distribution over the first six integer numbers which is generated by throws of a fair dice. Let x represent the set of possible outcomes, {1, 2, 3, 4, 5, 6} and p the associated probabilities {1/6, 1/6, 1/6, 1/6, 1/6, 1/6}; then the expected value or mean of x is $E(x) = \sum_i p_i x_i = 3.5$. This is an unconditional expectation. A condition expectation would be indicated by the notation $E(x|condition)$, such as $E(x \mid x$ is even$) = 4$. For our purposes the most important condition is the time at which the expectation was formed. For example, consider the expectation about next period's value of (the logarithm of) the general price level. This is conditional on the information available to the agent at the time he or she makes the expectation (or forecast), and would be denoted $E(p_{t+1} \mid \Omega_t)$ where Ω_t stands for the set of information available to the agent at time t. To streamline the notation somewhat this is usually expressed as $E_t(p_{t+1})$ where the subscript on the expectations operator indicates the set of information on which the forecast of the price level next period is based. The key implication about the rational expectations assumption is that while the agent's forecast may turn out to be inaccurate, any discrepancy at time $t+1$ between the forecast and the outturn, should not have been predictable at time t, i.e. the errors are not systematically related to any information available at time t. The error is a random variable, and the notion that it could not have been predicted means that its expected value (i.e. its mean), conditional on information available at time t, is zero: $E_t(p_{t+1} - E_t p_{t+1}) = 0$.

8.2   The Cagan model of inflation

This model is based on the demand for money. In normal circumstances the demand for real money balances increases with the volume of trans-actions and decreases with the nominal interest rate. The volume of transactions might be proxied by real gdp, and the nominal interest rate can be decomposed as the sum of the real interest rate and the expected rate of inflation. Then, adopting a simple linear form, we write the demand for money as: $m_t - p_t = \alpha_0 + \alpha_1(r_t + \pi^e_{t+1}) + \alpha_2 y_t + u_t$ where the money stock, m_t, the price level p_t and output y_t are measured in loga-rithms, r_t is the real interest rate, π^e_{t+1} is the expected rate of inflation and u_t is a random disturbance to money demand. But, as indicated in Section 7.4, since Cagan's model is designed to analyse inflation, and in particular high inflation, the real variables r_t and y_t are ignored or treated as constant, i.e. they are absorbed into the constant term, and the de-mand for real balances reduces to:

$$m_t - p_t = \alpha_0 - \alpha_1(E_t p_{t+1} - p_t) + u_t$$

where $\pi^e_{t+1} = E_t p_{t+1} - p_t$ and u_t is a random disturbance with mean equal to zero.

If the money supply m_t is exogenous, then this demand function for real balances determines the price level, and we can write down an expression for the (log of the) price level:

$$p_t = m_t - \alpha_0 + \alpha_1(E_t p_{t+1} - p_t) - u_t$$

$$p_t = \frac{m_t - \alpha_0 + \alpha_1 E_t p_{t+1} - u_t}{1 + \alpha_1} \tag{1}$$

Solving the model involves finding a solution for p_t which is con-sistent for $E_t p_{t+1}$. These are the endogenous variables in this system. The exogenous variables are m_t and u_t, so our solution for p_t will be in terms of m_t and u_t. But of course the time paths for p_t and $E_t p_{t+1}$ depend on what is assumed for the evolution of m_t. To be complete the model needs such an assumption. To solve the model with different money supply processes we apply the method of "undetermined coefficients" which can benefit from a flowgraph representation for explication. The procedure in the method of undetermined coefficients is first to assume the form of a solution—i.e. a linear model of the (logarithm of the) price level with particular exogenous variables—then to work out the details assuming that that form is correct, and finally to check that the solution is correct by inserting the derived expectations term into the original model. To illustrate, we consider the model with two different money supply processes.

(i)   **Money supply is constant, $m_t = \bar{m}$**

The model now comprises the two equations:

$$p_t = \frac{m_t - \alpha_0 + \alpha_1 E_t p_{t+1} - u_t}{1 + \alpha_1} \tag{1}$$

$$m_t = \bar{m} \tag{3}$$

from which we can see that the underlying determinants of p_t are a constant and the random term u_t, so we conjecture a solution which is a linear combination of these terms:

$$p_t = \delta_0 + \delta_1 u_t \tag{4}$$

in which δ_0 and δ_1 are the "undetermined coefficients". Now, assuming this conjecture is correct, we find the coefficients δ_0 and δ_1 in terms of the original parameters, α_0, α_1 and $\bar{m}$.   The conjecture implies $E_t p_{t+1} = \delta_0$ since $E_t u_{t+1} = 0$, and equating the right hand sides of our model equation (1) and its solution (4) gives:

$$(1+\alpha_1)^{-1}(\bar{m} - \alpha_0 + \alpha_1\delta_0 - u_t) = \delta_0 + \delta_1 u_t$$

To ensure this holds for all possible values of u_t, we equate the constant terms on both sides of the equation so that $(1+\alpha_1)^{-1}(\bar{m} - \alpha_0 + \alpha_1\delta_0) = \delta_0$, which implies that $\delta_0 = \bar{m} - \alpha_0$, and similarly we equate the coefficients of u_t so that $-(1+\alpha)^{-1} = \delta_1$, thereby deriving:

$$p_t = \bar{m} - \alpha_0 - u_t / (1+\alpha_1) \tag{5}$$

Now we check that this stochastic process for p_t is consistent with our original structural equation. Equation (5) implies

$$p_{t+1} = \bar{m} - \alpha_0 - u_{t+1}/(1+\alpha_1) \qquad \text{so} \qquad E_t p_{t+1} = \bar{m} - \alpha_0$$

and inserting this into our structural equation (1) reproduces the implied stochastic process (5). Thus we conclude that the price level fluctuates randomly around a constant value. The fact that the random term is multiplied by $-(1+\alpha_1)^{-1}$ implies that the variance of the random fluctuations is a decreasing function of the inflation semi-elasticity of demand for real balances, α_1 :

$$\text{var}(p) = (1+\alpha_1)^{-2}.\,\text{var}(u)$$

Now we develop the equivalent analysis in terms of flowgraphs. This is displayed in Figure 8.1. We start with the incomplete structural model of panel (i), which represents equations (1) and (3). The model is incomplete because it does not yet determine the endogenous expected price level next period, $E_t p_{t+1}$, which in the flowgraph seems to be an exogenous variable. Subsequent steps show how to make it endogenous. Panel (ii) shows the true reduced form of the model with its as yet unknown (i.e. undetermined) coefficients, while panel (iii) shifts the time forward one period to time $t+1$ and takes expectations as of the current period t. This provides the missing element to complete the structural form shown in panel (iv), for which the implied reduced form must be the same as that shown in panel (ii). Comparison between (iv) and (ii) enables the undetermined coefficients to be determined, yielding $\theta_0 = -1$, $\theta_1 = -(1+\alpha_1)^{-1}$ and $\theta_2 = 1$, as shown.

There are several points to note about this flowgraph representation and solution. First is the fact that the flowgraph represents the complete model of equations (1) and (2), including the constant terms α_0 and $\bar{m}$, which are treated as exogenous variables. This contrasts with the usual usual algebraic practice of treating the constant terms, as one combined constant. Instead separate undetermined coefficients are attached to both of these constant terms. Of course it is possible to mimic the usual algebraic treatment in a flowgraph setting, but the approach used here seems more natural. Thus the set of undetermined coefficients

(θ_0, θ_1 and θ_2) of the reduced form set out in part (ii) of Figure 8.1 is different from that of the earlier algebraic analysis (δ_0 and δ_1). This has no effect on the solution. Secondly, notice that the extra arcs created by the endogenization of the expected price level generate new paths but do not produce any loops.

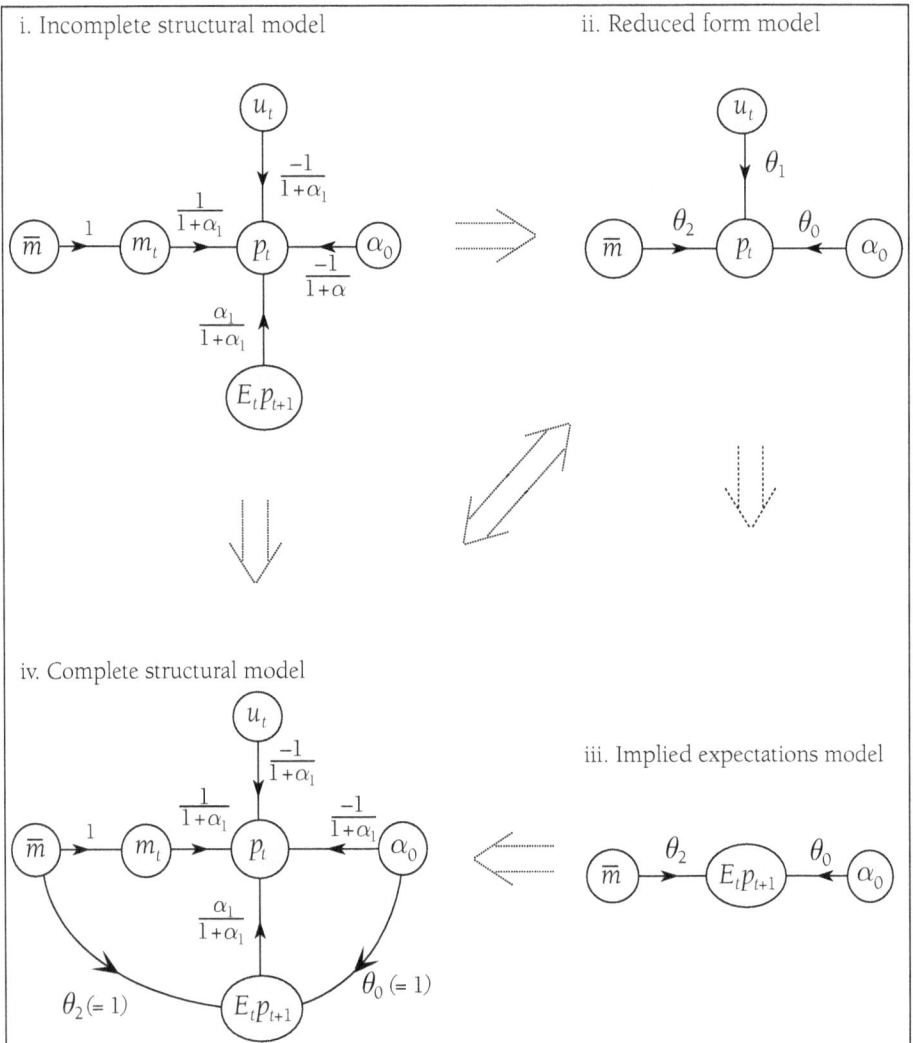

Figure 8.1 Flowgraph representation of the method of undetermined coefficients

(ii) Money supply follows a random walk with drift: $m_t = m_{t-1} + \mu + v_t$

This is a more credible model of an inflationary economy. The constant μ is the "drift" term; it corresponds to the average growth rate of the money supply. Random fluctuations in money growth are represented by the random variable v_t. Thus this period's (log) money supply is equal to last period's plus the drift term, which may be an expression of monetary policy, plus the random term. The model comprises this monetary growth process together with equation (1):

$$p_t = \frac{m_t - \alpha_0 + \alpha_1 E_t p_{t+1} - u_t}{1 + \alpha_1}$$

$$m_t = m_{t-1} + \mu + v_t ,$$

along with the assumption of rational expectations. It is represented in the flowgraph of Figure 8.2.

In Figure 8.2 the "incomplete structural model" is formed by the superposition of the graphs corresponding to these two equations. Again, it is "incomplete" because it does not yet incorporate the rational expectations assumption. However, the exogenous variables are identified, and that allows the reduced form of the model to be represented. The theta coefficients (transmittances) in the reduced form are not yet known, so these are the "undetermined coefficients". The reduced form is then subjected to the rational expectations assumption to derive the appropriate subgraph for the expected price level $E_t p_{t+1}$. The procedure here is to shift all the time subscripts of variables in the reduced form graph forward by one period, and then to take expectations as of time t. This causes the random variables to vanish because at time t they are forecast to be equal to zero (their mean values) in the next period. This gives the "implied expectations model". Now this is combined with the incomplete structural model by superposition in the usual way to give the "complete structural model". The undetermined coefficients are then obtained in terms of the model's parameters by equating path transmittances from all the exogenous variables to p_t in the "complete structural model" with those of the "reduced form model".

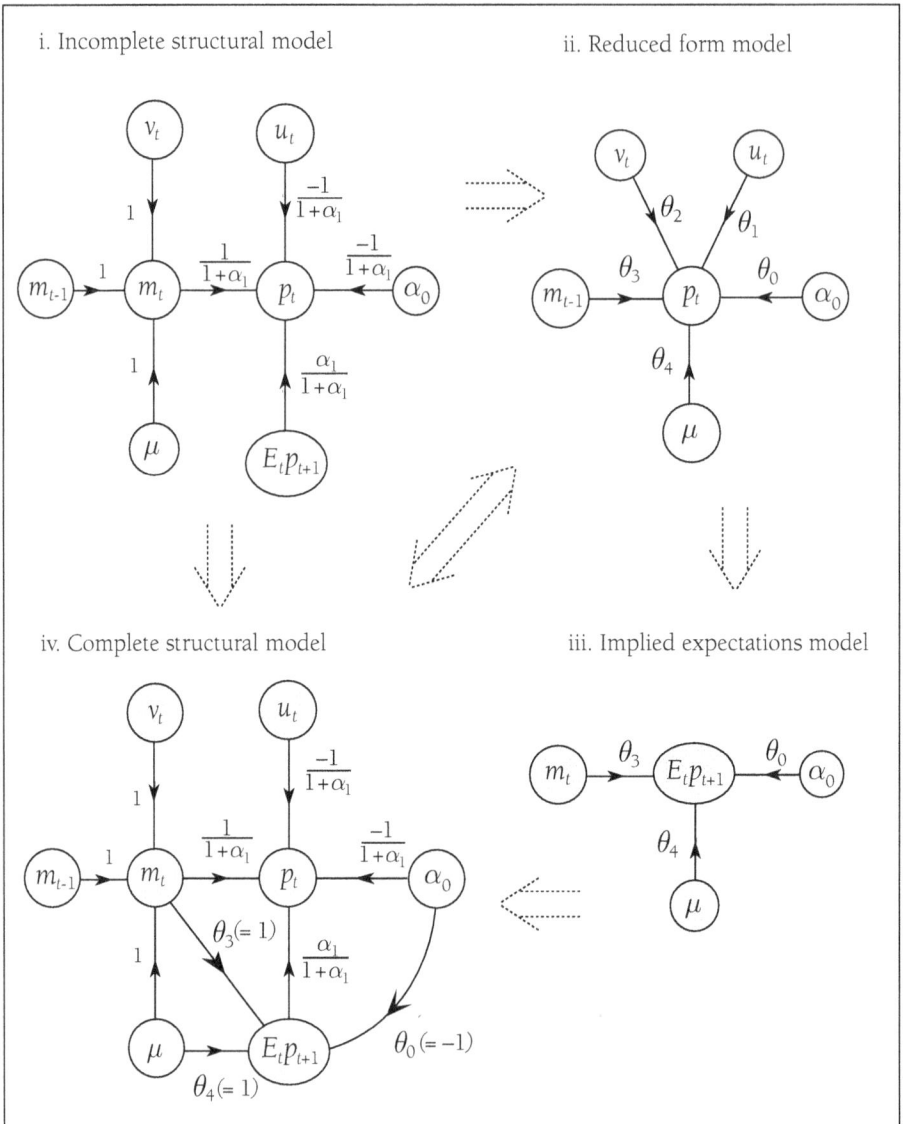

i. Incomplete structural model

ii. Reduced form model

iv. Complete structural model

iii. Implied expectations model

Figure 8.2 Solving the model with random growth in the money supply

Equating the path transmittances thus gives the following for the undetermined coefficients:

$$\theta_0 = \frac{1}{1+\alpha_1}(-1+\alpha_1\theta_0) \Rightarrow \theta_0 = -1$$

$$\theta_1 = \frac{-1}{1+\alpha_1}$$

$$\theta_3 = \frac{1}{1+\alpha_1}(1+\alpha_1\theta_3) \Rightarrow \theta_3 = 1$$

$$\theta_2 = \frac{1}{1+\alpha_1}(1+\alpha_1\theta_3) \Rightarrow \theta_2 = 1$$

$$\theta_4 = \frac{1}{1+\alpha_1}(1+\alpha_1\theta_3 + \alpha_1\theta_4) \Rightarrow \theta_4 = 1+\alpha_1$$

Hence the reduced form equation for the logarithm of the price level is:

$$p_t = -\alpha_0 + m_{t-1} + (1+\alpha_1)\mu + v_t - u_t /(1+\alpha_1)$$

or: $$p_t = -\alpha_0 + m_t + \alpha_1\mu + v_t - u_t /(1+\alpha_1)$$

Thus proportional shocks to money supply (v_t) increase the price level one for one, and positive shocks to money demand (u_t) have a negative effect on the price level which is less than one for one unless the demand for real money balances is insensitive to expected inflation (i.e. $\alpha_1=0$). Abstracting from the random fluctuations implied by u_t and v_t, the price level moves in parallel with the path of money supply, and the rate of growth of money supply also affects the price level. It can be seen that the model of the previous section with constant money supply is a special case of this model, with $\mu = v_t = 0$.

8.3   Aggregate supply and demand

Here we take the AS-AD model presented in Section 7.5 and replace the expectations formation assumptions used there by the assumption of rational expectations. The model has no stochastic components, but what is of particular interest is how the methodology of rational expectations influences the structure of the model. The equations of the AS-AD model are repeated here for convenience.

$$y^S = y^* + \beta(p - p^e)$$ AS

$$y^D = A - \varphi p \qquad\qquad\qquad \text{AD}$$

$$\Delta p = \delta(y^D - y^S) \qquad\qquad\qquad \text{inflation}$$

Now these equations themselves imply the p^e variable, reflecting the self-referential character of models with rational expectations. This incomplete structural model is presented as a flowgraph in Figure 8.3. It is as yet incomplete because the rational expectations assumption has not been incorporated into the model. To facilitate manipulation of this model, it is also presented in a condensed form which shows only the "exogenous variables" (including p^e) and the price level to reduce unnecessary clutter.

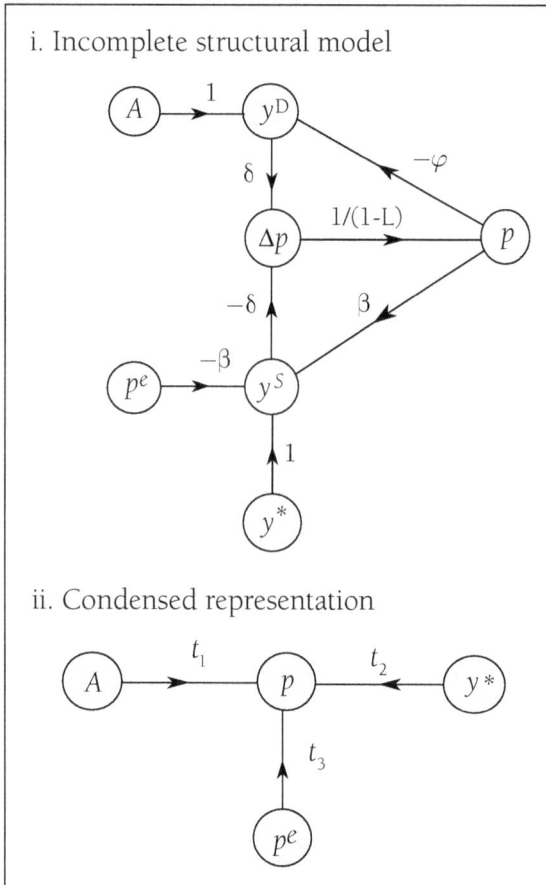

Figure 8.3 Incomplete structural AS-AD model

The transmittances of the condensed model, obtained from graph reduction or from Mason's rule, are:

$$t_1 = \frac{\delta}{1-L+\beta\delta+\varphi\delta} \ ; \ \ t_2 = \frac{-\delta}{1-L+\beta\delta+\varphi\delta} \ ; \ \ t_3 = \frac{\beta\delta}{1-L+\beta\delta+\varphi\delta} \ .$$

The condensed model is now the object of the method of undetermined coefficients set out in the previous section. The steps in this procedure are as before: first to write down the reduced form of the model, recognising that p^e is endogenous; secondly to take expectations; and thirdly to superimpose this expectational model on the condensed structural form. This enables the new unknown path transmittances—the "undetermined coefficients"—to be evaluated in terms of the original parameters of the model by equating the transmittances of the reduced form with those of the complete (condensed) structural form. All this is shown in Figure 8.4.

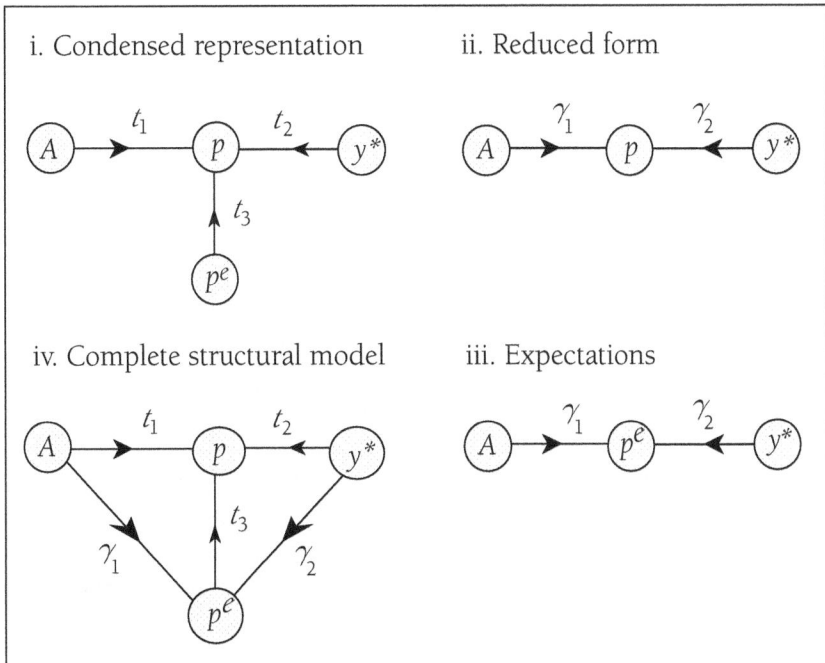

Figure 8.4 Graphs for the method of undetermined coefficients

The undetermined coefficients γ_1 and γ_2 are thus:

$$\gamma_1 = t_1 + \gamma_1 t_3 \to \gamma_1 = \frac{t_1}{1-t_3} \to \gamma_1 = \frac{\delta}{1-L+\varphi\delta}$$

and $\qquad \gamma_2 = t_2 + \gamma_2 t_3 \to \gamma_2 = \frac{t_2}{1-t_3} \to \gamma_2 = -\frac{\delta}{1-L+\varphi\delta}$.

Finally the full model can be displayed after reinstating the detail that was suppressed at the outset.

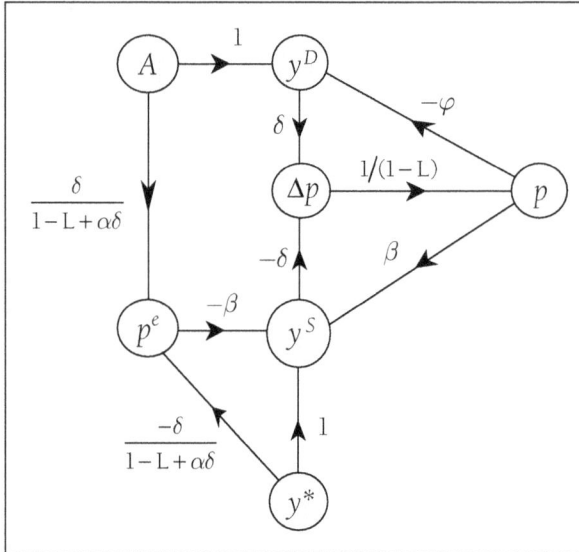

Figure 8.5 The full structural model

If we calculate the transmittances from the exogenous variables to the endogenous variables in this model we find them to be identical with those of the perfect foresight model of Section 7.5. This should be no surprise because rational expectations in the absence of an unpredictable stochastic element in the model is equivalent to perfect foresight. This means that there is never a discrepancy between the expected price level and the actual price level, so the corresponding term in the aggregate supply function is always zero, and the system never departs from the natural rate of output. Thus the system remains on the vertical long-run aggregate supply schedule (in P-y space) in the short-run as well as the long-run. In order for the upward-sloping short-run aggregate supply function to play any role, it is necessary to introduce a random term into the model so that future outcomes are not completely predictable.

Exercise 19

i. Use Mason's rule to confirm that the transmittances from A to p and from A to p^e are exactly equal in the flowgraph of Figure 8.5.

ii. Show further that the response of p (and p^e) to a step change in A is gradual and monotonic,

iii. Show that y^s moves in lock step with y^*.

Appendix

Computer Modelling of Flowgraphs[†]

While formulating, manipulating and solving small flowgraphs on paper is straightforward and insightful, it can nevertheless be very helpful to have a patient and capable machine assistant to remove the drudgery, avoid mistakes and save on paper. Here we describe such a computer application which enables flowgraph modelling on a screen. This software is freely available as an internet application, used as a Java applet within a web browser. What follows is an outline of how to make use of this tool.

The program can be accessed at the following web address:

`http://www.geoffwyatt.com/flowgraphs/`

When the applet is loaded, a blank screen appears with a toolbar header. There are three "modes of operation" represented by the cluster of three icons on the left of the toolbar: *node creation*, *arc creation* and *transmittance measurement*.

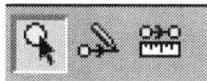

The other icons on the toolbar are *scissors* for deleting selected objects, a *reversing arrow* for causality reversal (this should be treated with care), an *undo and redo* pair of icons, and a *loop-reckoner*.

The program opens in *node creation* mode. To create a layout of **nodes**, double-click in various places in the blank area. When a hexago-

---

[†] The computer program described here was written by Thomas K. Wyatt.

nal node appears you can give it a label from the keyboard. Double-clicking on the node allows you to rename it. Click-drag moves the node.

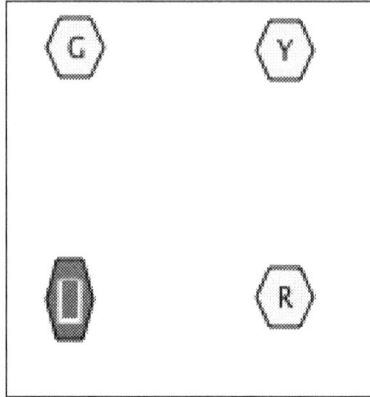

To create **arcs** you may <u>either</u>:

(i) Switch to *arc creation* mode (click the middle icon of the cluster of three on the left of the toolbar) and connect pairs of nodes by click-dragging; or

(ii) Remain in *node creation* mode and RightClick-Drag (on a PC) or Control-Click-Drag (on a Mac) to connect pairs of nodes.

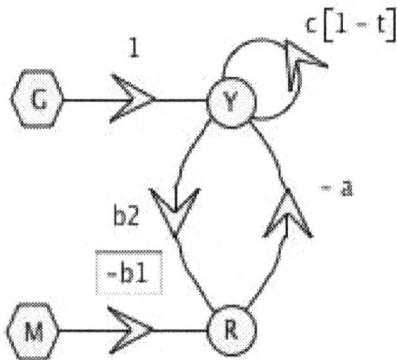

Move arcs by click-dragging on an arrowhead. The default arc transmittance is 1. It can be changed by double-clicking the existing transmittance, and its position near the arrowhead can be changed by click-dragging. A **self-loop** is created if an arc is drawn from a node back to itself.

Exogenous nodes remain as hexagons; endogenous nodes are circles. If you draw another (forward or reverse) connection between two nodes that are already connected, then one arc may be drawn on top of the other. Simply click-drag the arrowhead to separate them.

Click-dragging from an empty point on the screen will **mark** all those parts of the flowgraph enclosed by the cursor-created rectangle. These can now **move as a group** on click-dragging, remaining locked together.

To **delete** a node or an arc, click on it and use the *scissors* on the toolbar.

To **absorb** a node, Right-click (PC) or Command-click (Mac) on the node and select "Eliminate Node" from the contextual menu. The flowgraph will change as a result, creating new arcs, and may need to be rearranged. This operation, and all others above, can be reversed with the *undo/redo* button on the toolbar.

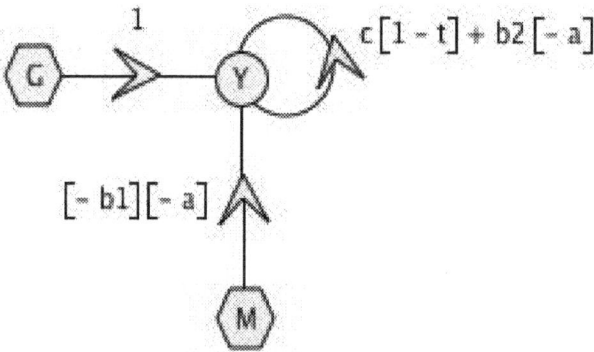

The R node has been absorbed

A table of **loops** and the **system determinant** are displayed in a separate box when you click on the *loop-reckoner* button. Passing the cursor over these items in the box causes the relevant loop on the flowgraph to be emboldened.

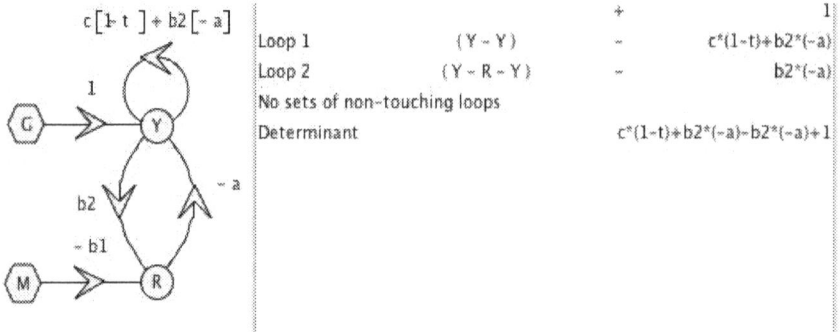

			+	1
Loop 1	(Y ~ Y)		~	c*(1~t)+b2*(~a)
Loop 2	(Y ~ R ~ Y)		~	b2*(~a)
No sets of non~touching loops				
Determinant				c*(1~t)+b2*(~a)~b2*(~a)+1

$$c[1\text{-}t]+b2[\text{-}a]$$

Loops identified and system determinant calculated

To measure **transmittances** click on the *transmittance measurement* button on the toolbar (it shows a tape measure below two connected nodes) and then click-drag from the originating node to the destination node. Note that it only makes sense to calculate a transmittance from an exogenous to an endogenous node. You may find that the transmittances (including loop transmittances) may not be expressed in the simplest form—it is up to the user to do any algebraic simplifications. The measurement arrow can be dragged to a more convenient location on the screen if desired. Double-clicking on the measurement arrow pulls up a separate box which shows how the transmittance is composed of path transmittances and co-factors from non-touching loops.

$$\frac{1}{1 - b2\left[\text{~}a\right] - c\left[1 \text{~} t\right]}$$

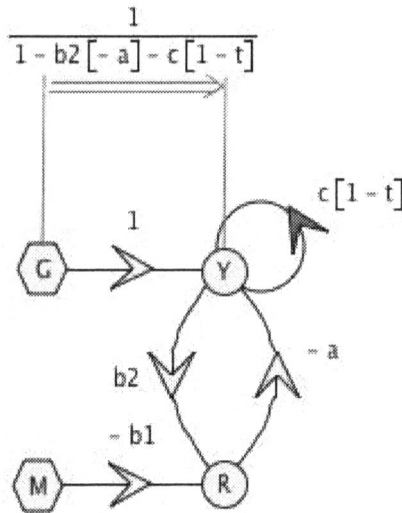

Note that the graphs you create cannot be saved or copied as manipulatable objects, though you can save them, frozen, as picture files with a screen- or window-capture utility—*i.e.* in Windows use the PrintScreen or Cntrl-PrintScreen command from the keyboard, or in Mac OSX use the "Grab" application. The picture can then be pasted into another application like a paint program or a word processor. To **print out**, again use a screen- or window-capture utility.

www.ingramcontent.com/pod-product-compliance
Lightning Source LLC
Chambersburg PA
CBHW031944190326
41519CB00007B/657